Fashion and Clothing Technology

IVY NELMS, A.C.I.
Lecturer at the London College of Fashion

HULTON EDUCATIONAL PUBLICATIONS

ISBN 0 7175 0682 7

First published 1976 by
Hulton Educational Publications Ltd.,
Raans Road, Amersham, Bucks.

Filmset and printed in Great Britain by
BAS Printers Limited, Wallop, Hampshire

INTRODUCTION

This book has been written with the aim of encouraging you not only to master the techniques described in these pages, but also to keep developing your skills. Basic principles are given for the main aspects of clothing manufacture – design, textiles, pattern drafting and cutting and making up. The author has borne in mind the needs of the CSE and GCE student and the technical student intending to enter the trade or make a career in the fashion world.

The questions, projects and notes are intended to guide you and make you keen to widen your knowledge. Fashion itself is ever-changing, never static, and it demands that those who specialise in it are likewise versatile, forward-looking and always seeking to increase their creative potential.

After studying this book you will be aware of the high degree of skill and satisfaction to be gained from the arts of dressmaking, pattern-cutting and designing and also of the excellent prospects in the fashion and clothing field.

ACKNOWLEDGEMENTS

I should like to record my thanks to the following for their help in preparing the book:
Veronica Marsh for the cover design; P. Kerr-Cross, Janina Orzioro, Dian Bibby, Dorothy Ralphs, G. J. Galsworthy, Peggy Lim and Sylvia Lim for illustrations; R. Downs; R. Baines; Singer Sewing Machine Co. Ltd.; Viking Sewing Machine Co.; I.C.I. Fibres Ltd.; Courtaulds Ltd.; Eastman Machine Co. Ltd.; Thomas Beecroft & Co. Ltd.; E. Alexander & Co. Ltd.; Perivale Sewing Silks. Finally I must thank my dear daughter-in-law for her patience in typing and re-typing my manuscript.

Ivy Nelms

CONTENTS

PART 1 DESIGN

Fashions Through the Ages

Style lines

Fashion as we know it today is greatly influenced by styles worn in the past. Clothes, after all, are part of the continuing pattern of life through different periods of history, and it is natural that fashion designers in their search for new ideas should often turn to the past.

If you are imaginative and have a knowledge of historical costume, you will be able to trace the origins of many of the fashionable garments worn today. Practically every garment you see has in some way been styled before. Fashions come and go and styles change when people tire of the clothes they wear. In mediaeval times styles altered only slowly, as there was little money to buy new clothes. It is only since the nineteenth century, with the general increase in prosperity and the coming of machines to replace hand tailoring, that changes in fashion have become rapid.

At present we are in a period of history unrivalled for the versatility and variety of clothes. It is a wonderful time in which to enjoy and wear whatever suits you and whatever you like. There is no need to conform strictly with fashion. You wear what *you* think is suitable for the occasion – and this can be anything today.

To be in London and see the many types of garments is an education in itself. But that applies to most large cities and at times it is fun just to stand and look – and, if possible, quickly sketch the styles around you.

Look carefully at the various silhouettes sketched on the following pages. See whether you can detect any of the basic cuts of the past used in garments worn today.

Inspiration for style lines

Fashion is a continuous cycle and a large number of today's ideas are derived from 'Old Masters'.

It is said that Christian Dior, a well known French couturier whose name, together with the House of Dior, still exists today, used to get much of his inspiration from old paintings.

If you read the life stories of many of the notable fashion designers you will discover that their fame began with ideas gathered from museums and art galleries.

Films based on authentic happenings in history have made millions of people familiar with the dress of other times. Many of the styles have been copied, adapted and used by the clothing industry. And in this way other fashions have been created for a while.

Can you think which period of history inspired the long boots, the tunic tops and the mini – or from what period the idea for maxi skirts, boots, cloaks and fur hoods and long jackets came – or even in which films these were shown? All clothes can be traced to their origins and we find many ideas from costumes used in the Far East, Middle Europe and Russia incorporated into the styling of today.

Historical Costume as it Affects Today's Fashions

Distinguishing various periods

Each change of fashion, then, can be recognised as some revival from the past when similar clothes were once worn. From the earliest days, when someone made a coat of many colours for Joseph, the world has been full of the sound of the cutting and clipping of scissors.

The history of fashion is marked by the spirit of each succeeding age, although distinctive styles for certain trades and professions can be seen in the dress of those who followed them for many generations.

Quiz

Can you think of any garments symbolising particular trades or professions that have been in existence for generations?

Julius Caesar was recognised by his toga and Queen Elizabeth I by the Piccadilly ruff. What was typical of Henry VIII? Which clothes do you associate with Napoleon? What was characteristic of Sir Walter Raleigh? And how would you have recognised Samuel Pepys – or Dapper Dick, as he signed himself?

Research

Arrange visits to art galleries where you can discover a wealth of information from the many artists of bygone years who portrayed people in the clothes of their time.

You can also learn a great deal from museums, especially where authentic costumes are on display, as in the Victoria and Albert Museum, London. Observe the beautiful handwork and materials used at different periods. Make a list of the various sewing and embroidery stitches and compare it with those commonly used in the clothing industry today. You will be surprised at the result.

Old Family Pictures
Old photographs can be most valuable, especially if they are from a family album. It is hard to believe that the parents and grandparents of today wore such peculiar clothes. Magazines and old newspapers are another valuable source of information.

Brasses in Churches
Many monuments and old brasses you find in churches illustrate the costumes of past centuries. If you can get permission, take brass rubbings, and these too will help your researches.

Questions

1 Before the Roman invasion what did a British chieftain's dress consist of?

2 What did the ordinary tribesman of that time wear?

3 After the Roman invasion Britons who desired to cultivate their taste adopted the . . . . . ?

4 What did the Romans adopt from the British?

5 What was the distinguishing head dress for the ladies in 800?

6 In the year 1100 what dress did the ladies wear?

7 What do you notice about the dress in 1300?

8 Can you describe the dresses worn by the wives of Henry VIII?

9 Mention one historical film you have seen and comment on the costumes.

10 Do you think fashions changed in Elizabeth I's reign? If so, what were the most prominent features in your opinion?

11 When were flesh-coloured stockings first introduced?

12 When did women in their ordinary daytime fashions first reveal their legs below the knees?

Project

Sketch and then make in half-scale (or full scale) what you could have worn two hundred years ago, if you were fourteen years old.

Discover what clothes were worn by (i) a peasant and (ii) a baron during the Hundred Years War.

What did a peasant boy and girl wear during the time of the Plague and how did a courtier dress at that period?

Make a detailed list of the underwear used by the ladies from the time of Elizabeth I to Elizabeth II. Give details of the materials used.

If you have a good knowledge of historical costume, sketch some garments worn at the present time that are replicas of past fashions.

Some outer garments of today derive from the past. Write a list of these and illustrate the types of the materials used.

Costume Cavalcade of this Century

When you feel you have studied sufficiently the costumes of the past, take a more detailed look at this century. See how after the First World War Chanel changed women's clothes. Then, in the thirties, garments became more intricate in cut, while evening dresses became voluminous. Note how, during the Second World War, clothes became simple again, until Christian Dior launched the New Look in the forties.

FASHIONS IN THE 1940'S

FASHIONS IN
THE 1970'S

The Study of Design

The fashion industry

Fashion is a very serious business, although the word 'fashion' conjures up visions of frivolous and gimmicky garments. People in the industry are essentially technical and it is a very demanding trade which requires skills of a very high order, hard work and the flair to create something different, yet suitable to the mood of the moment. A dress does not necessarily have to be gimmicky, although in every collection you will find a garment which has an unusual feature – perhaps a decoration or ornament or just a 'crazy' garment. These creations have great news values for firms and add fun to the collection. But they are not the garments that usually sell well, unless they are the start of a fashion trend. The classical garments are often known as the 'bread and butter' of the trade and consequently bring in more sales than many of the more startling lines.

Designing dresses

Most people can design clothes. It is so simple to look through books and say 'I will have the collar of this style, and the bodice of that and sleeves from another'. This is a form of permutation. By adapting garments in this way hundreds of styles can be evolved. Many large manufacturing firms do this with several of their garments, known as classical garments. They alter the cloths, trimmings and length (according to the current fashion trend) and so are able to use the main basic pattern time and again. If you merely did fashion permutations it would not necessarily mean that you would be a good designer. To design well you need to have a knowledge of fashion and to be able to make up garments, to have good taste and instinctive flair for colour, cloth textures and the ability to sense what is right for the times.

Be practical

A good design must always be a practical design. The sketch must be distinct and show every working detail so that the pattern cutter cannot be misled when converting the idea into a practical form. It must be *functional* – that is, the garment should be easy to get on and off and there should not be any restriction in any part of it.

The wholesale trade

The majority of the skilled people in this trade are most enthusiastic about their work. They seem to extract from it sheer enjoyment. Maybe it is because they are always creating and doing something different, for every day work alters in the fashion trade. Fashions change, materials differ, styles alter, machines are different, while techniques become more advanced all the time. This is a very competitive industry where firms vie with one another quite ruthlessly. Ideas are kept as secret as possible, so that until they are produced no one else will have the opportunity of copying the original. This is especially evident in the couture houses, where every sketch is carefully guarded until after the collection is shown.

Design qualifications

If you want to be a designer, ask yourself whether you have the following qualifications:
A retentive memory: are you able to retain pictures in your mind of garments you have seen?
A keen eye for detail, to remember shapes, trimmings, decorations, ornaments etc.
A colour sense and love of materials.
Appreciation of a line.
Common sense and sound practical judgement.

Ask yourself whether you are capable of coping with failures and disappointments. A designer cannot give up easily, as the clothing trade is most competitive and ruthless.

You notice that an ability to draw is not featured in the list. This is an asset if you have it, but the lack of it will not be too much of a drawback. If you can provide good working sketches with written information and details you can still produce wonderful designs. After all, designing is a three-dimensional art and so one must also think of forms and figures 'in the round' as creations take shape.

The following books are recommended for beginners:

The Technique of Dress Design by Brenda Naylor, Batsford, 1966

Fashion Design Drawing by Patrick John Ireland, Batsford, 1970

The Diagrammatic Form

Shaping for the figure

Start to draw a figure by copying the diagrammatic form illustrated. As you draw, try to visualise the shapings of the figure, get movement into the body if you can, by re-positioning the head, arms and legs. Remember, a body is three-dimensional and does not have straight lines. A body is curved and rounded. Because of this, material draped around a body will press against the most protruding parts. These are the bust points. Above and below these prominent parts wedges of material need to be taken into darts or pleats to fit around the curves and to give shape to the figure. The material must not be stretched and needs to be shaped, but without restricting breathing or movement. Shapings for the body are made in many ways, by seams, darts, tucks, folds, pleats, gathers and flares. They can be found above and below the shoulder blades at the back, at the side body (to fit over the hip muscles), under the bust and at the elbow and shoulder points. These shapings can be made at any position around the point of the bulge.

10

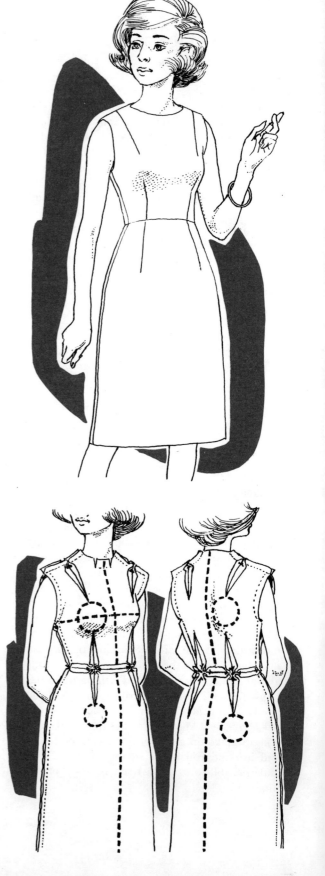

Creating different shapings

Look in fashion magazines and see how designers have created shape in various ways for the most prominent parts of the body. You see how shapings can be made into different designs, as provision is made for the bust by (1) soft folds (2) gathers (3) seam lines.

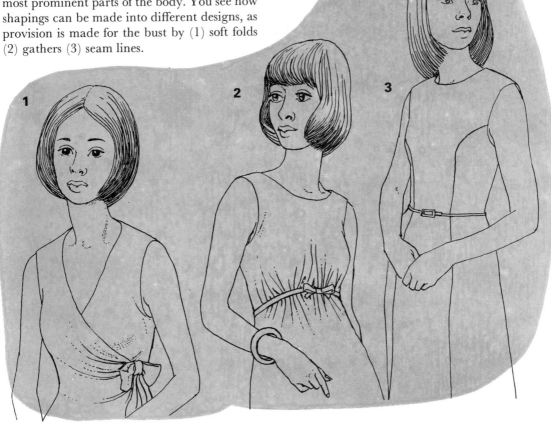

What to do

Copy the diagrammatic form on page 10 or sketch a basic body shape and begin creating dress styles.

Design six dresses with different necklines and sleeve lengths, but with the basic darts in the side seam and under the bust, keeping a straight silhouette.

Look at the original garments designed as shown in the illustrations, re-position the darts, taking into consideration the shapings of the necklines and alter the lengths to suit the necklines.

Design six straight dresses, positioning a *horizontal* seam across the body, adjusting necklines and sleeve lengths accordingly.

Design six straight garments, positioning *vertical* seams down the body. Watch your propor-

tions in the beginning and try to get movement into your drawings. Show the garment to the best advantage and rough in the figures inside the clothes. Keep a sharp point on your pencil and do not be scared to rub out things that are wrong. Use as long lines as possible and to fix a knowledge of proportion in your head, try sketching from life.

Constantly look at feet, hands, face, etc. and compare them with one another. In this way you will become familiar with the relative sizes of each part of the body. The most useful rule of proportion is that of the head to the body. It is usual to assume that *eight head lengths go into the rest of the body for an adult*. Of course, this does not always apply to the ordinary individual, but is a good basis for designers.

The Silhouette

The outline of the garment

The main basic silhouettes throughout the generations have been the *tubular*, the *bell* and the *bustle*.

Within the last few years there has been a constant change of silhouettes and today more

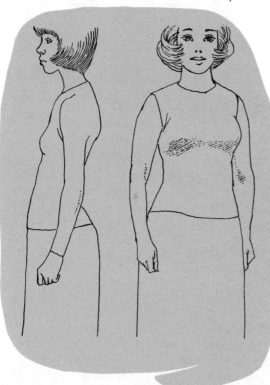

than one is fashionable at the same time.

The silhouette defines the shape made and reveals the waist placement, the skirt length, the sleeve contours and conveys a first impression of the garment.

Look carefully at these shapes and then, using the sketches previously made, change them into first the *bell* and then the *bustle*. Afterwards create your own version of a silhouette.

Individual shapes or silhouettes

When designing for an individual you must take the whole personality of the wearer into account. Observe the manner and the general bearing of a person and then keep in mind the following points:

1 Emphasise the best lines of a person's figure.
2 Disguise the least attractive.
3 See that the lines are in proportion to the figure.
4 For the angular figure remember that curved lines have a softening effect.
5 For the plump person avoid bouffant styles and stiff stand-away effects. (Straight lines, neither too tight or too loose are suitable.)
6 For the tall, thin woman, loose lines are best.

Complete this list with your own comments concerning the silhouette desired for the small plump person.

Then produce a sketch of a silhouette you feel would be most suitable for:

(a) yourself (b) your mother (c) your grandmother.

Dress Styles

Familiar dress styles

Dress styles are the lines that distinguish one shape from another. You have seen shirtwaister styles, cardigan styles, sheath styles, shift and sack. They are the details produced within the basic shapes. The shirtwaister, cardigan and princess are repeatedly used in collections and are typical classical garments.

Can you think of any other dress styles apart from those illustrated?

Style lines

Lines can be used in a garment to make you look thinner, fatter, shorter, taller or heavier. Skilful use of lines can create visual illusions with any part of the body you wish to emphasise. They can follow the shape of the body or be in contrast to the shape. The lines determine the silhouette and within the outline of the figure, shapes can be created. Lines can be straight, curved, diagonal, horizontal or vertical.

Vertical lines give a slender effect, provided that they are not repeated in quantity. Horizontal lines usually add width to the figure. Diagonal lines are pleasing to the eye if used as a subtle slant, but they can be broadening if used indiscriminately. The degree of slant determines the illusion.

It is said that line gives length in the direction in which it runs. Have you noticed how the eye has the tendency to follow lines? Look at the sketches illustrated. Which line does your eye follow?

The direction of a line can be emphasised by the use of trimmings or contrasts or by the fabric texture. As a designer you must not always adhere to the traditional pattern of lines. Experiment and rethink and look at the work of recent fashion designers. Many have ignored traditional principles of line and created something quite startling and new.

Can you think of a designer who has ignored traditional lines?

Camouflaging the figure

The fabric itself may provide the main interest and draw attention away from the figure faults, and many materials can be used with this in mind. To increase size, large checks or stripes are used. To decrease size, small patterns and darker colours are suitable, while a combination of plain and patterned fabrics can camouflage faults in the figure.

All objects grow smaller in size as they become more distant. Imagine that you are standing in the middle of a railway track, as level as a sheet of water. You will observe that the rails stretch away into the distance, becoming smaller and smaller and closer together, until they meet, then at the level of your eye they disappear as a point on the sky-line. The place where they meet is the 'vanishing-point' or 'centre of vision'.

It is essential that you practise drawing in perspective as this plays a great part in designing garments. The positioning of pockets, seam lines and buttons can be affected and it is always advisable to look at your garment in a mirror before finally deciding on button placements and pocket details. Imagine how ridiculous a 7 cm square pocket would look if applied to a 96 cm hip. In other words, it would be out of proportion to the rest of the garment. Apart from looking peculiar, the added part would be neither useful nor decorative.

Although as a general rule one needs to recognise proportion as something vital in good design, it is worth noticing that many designers in the last few years have defied this principle.

Can you give examples of garments which in your opinion were disproportionate and yet were most popular?

Collect examples of pictures depicting badly designed garments and see what you can do to improve them.

Be discreet – do not use too many lines. Take into consideration the material and the proportions of a person.

16

Colour

Just think how important colour is, not only in the clothes we wear but in our homes and our surroundings, our pleasures and entertainments. Colour is with us all the time – dull, interesting, bright, pleasant, harmonious, garish or faded. In early times men painted their bodies with dyes from plants. Even today Scottish plaids still identify the different clans and colour has an important role in the world of sport where it picks out the members of opposing teams.

Think of the wonderful combinations and variations of tone you can find in present-day materials. Colour is of the utmost importance and plays a vital part in the design of clothes.

Primary colours

The primary colours red, blue and yellow are combined to produce the secondary colours:

Red and blue produce violet.

Blue and yellow produce green.

Red and yellow produce orange.

Colour used incorrectly in clothes can make them much less attractive. For instance, the eye can quickly travel from one area to another and the use of too many colours will make a garment look like a rainbow.

Effects of colour

Colour can be either warm or cool. Red, orange and yellow are classed as warm colours. Cool colours are blue and violet. Green comes between warm and cool.

Warm colours produce an illusion of greater emphasis and call attention to the body size and contours. Cool colours produce the illusion of less importance and minimise the contours and shapings of the body.

Questions

1 Give six examples of coloured uniforms used to identify their wearers.

2 Emotions are expressed with colour. Give examples, e.g. *in the pink*, *feeling blue*, *black with rage*, *green with envy*.

3 Write down your colour preferences and draw three garments combining two or more of these colours in a style.

4 Do bright, high-toned colours make the figure appear larger?

5 Weak colours are less conspicuous. What would they do to a figure?

6 A general rule is that bright colours should be used sparingly and less intense colours used in large areas. What is your opinion?

7 Does the light under which a colour is viewed affect the depth of the colour or not?

8 What are pigmental colours?

9 What are sombre colours?

10 Do colours affect each other?

11 What are neutral colours?

12 If the eye looks at a bright colour persistently, then afterwards at a white sheet of paper, an after-image of the object invariably appears. Experiment with red and see what results. Write down your observations, then compare with someone else's results.

Texture

A garment should express a theme and all the parts that are used to make the garment should be in harmony. The original idea can be lost if, for instance, proper proportions are not observed when using coloured sections or different textured fabrics. Texture alters colour because it absorbs light differently. A shiny fabric such as satin, although dyed the same colour as a woollen gabardine, would look different in shade. This is why it is always difficult to match accessories with various fabrics.

Fabric texture should be related to the design and to the purpose and time at which the garment is to be worn.

The texture of clothes can affect the result a designer wishes to achieve, so careful consideration must be given to the selection. Owing to light reflection, some fabrics can produce the illusion either of increasing the figure proportions or of decreasing them.

Questions

1 'Styling and texture need to walk hand in hand'. What is your opinion? Does it apply today?
2 We live in an age of strong contrasts. Give three examples of strong contrasts that are accepted in clothes today which a few years ago might have been considered in 'bad taste'.
3 Would you say that the following textures harmonise? Group together any you think are compatible: lace (fine), chiffon, nylon, silk, tweed, jerseys, firm velvet and worsted, soft velvet and crêpe, suede.

Project

Make a list of contrasts to go with the following colours: black, white, grey, red, orange, yellow, green, blue and violet.

Make yourself a colour chart, starting with the primary colours followed by the secondaries and then adding all the complementaries.

Collect six swatches of different coloured materials. Match these materials with linings, cottons and ribbons and notice the variation in the shades. Write your comments on the different textures.

The texture of the cloth

Some materials speak for themselves and then the choice of the design for the cloth is immediately obvious to a designer. It is good, however, to observe the following rule: *heavily and large patterned materials are best when used for uncomplicated designs*. This applies to velvets, as intricate seamings break up the surface of the cloth and the beauty is lost. Good, simple lines are needed for all patterned cloths. Unpleasing effects can be obtained with plaids and checks if there are too many seams to break the continuity of the plaid pattern.

The design and texture of the cloth can affect the appearance of a garment enormously. Textures and colours have periods of popularity, but there are some textures that remain popular year after year and are usually neither rough nor very smooth. Dress-weight linen and flannel are two good examples. Fabrics with a piled surface such as velvet, velours and corduroy, reflect and absorb light and are known as the shiny textures. Satin is a good example and it is very figure-revealing.

When deciding which material and texture to use, lay the cloths across the shoulders near the face and look into a long mirror to see the effect they produce.

Many designers prefer to select their material first, as the texture and pattern of the cloth determines the design and the occasion when the garment will be worn. The 'handle' of the cloth decides whether it is suitable for draping, pleats, folds, or tucks. Firmly woven fabrics tend to be made into tailored styles, while soft, easily draped fabrics are used for more feminine garments.

At present we are in a period which defies tradition and adventurous designers have been known to use bold contrasts. However, fine sheer fabrics go well with lace, embroidery, sequins, silks, satins and taffetas for formal evening wear; long tweed skirts and heavier materials would be appropriate for the more casual evening wear which has become popular now. If *style lines* are to dominate, then the material should be plain. If the *fabric* is to be important, the design lines need to be simple.

Age Group

Many firms have an 'image', and it may be Outsize, Teenagers, Couture, Trendy or some other specialised market.

Firms who have an image also know the colours the customers will expect from the manufacturers each season and these colours usually feature in each collection.

Current fashion trend

Do not be too far ahead of current fashion and certainly do not lag behind it. Consider also whether you are dealing with a garment which can be mass-produced easily for the wholesale trade. Buyers are, to a certain extent, influenced by what has gone before. But be guided by your own instinct if you have a fashion flair. Remember that the designing of winter clothes often has to be done in the previous spring, so it is wise to be up to date.

Questions

1 What firms sponsor Crimplene, Liberty prints and Banlon?
2 What are the current fashion colours?
3 When would you use easy-care materials such as drip-dry, crease-resistant cloths?
4 What designs would you use for stretch fabrics?
5 What materials would you suggest for casual wear?
6 Design a dress for a soft jersey fabric.
7 Design a dress in velvet material.
8 Design a two-piece in a tweed cloth, medium weight.
9 Collect six examples of materials and design according to the cloth you have selected.
10 Name six firms who, in your opinion, have an image. Describe it briefly.
11 Name four companies noted for their particular fabrics and styling.

Designing for Wholesale Manufacturing and Individual Figures

Working sketches

However clumsy your sketches may appear to you, they are your only means of recording the ideas that come and go so quickly. It is not advisable to depend upon even the best of memories for retaining some striking detail. Keep a notebook in your bag or pocket as you travel around and record anything that attracts you and is suitable to be adapted into a style. But do not be content with poor sketches. Practise drawing whenever possible and you will soon evolve a style of your own. A designer must be sufficiently down-to-earth to produce sketches that can be carried out in three-dimensional form. In other words, from the designs must come patterns which are practical enough to translate into mass-production terms. They must be designs which will sell – which means they must be reasonably attractive and exciting, but they must also be practical from the manufacturing point of view. Many sketches are produced with no indication of the darts, the final seams, the back of the garment or the placement of openings. Consequently they leave a pattern cutter in a quandary as to how to make a garment functional while keeping exactly to the sketch. If your sketch is to have character, let it also show your impression of the prevailing fashion. To do this you must emphasise the silhouette.

Figure height

Do not make the figures too tall; make them slightly above average height. (Many pattern cutting scales are based on the 'eight heads' theory.) The reason for making the sketch a little taller is that it makes the garment look more elegant. Do not try to achieve originality by making the garment look outrageous and ridiculous. Try to imagine the person wearing the garment and whether it would make her more attractive.

Conveying your first impression

The garment silhouette is vital if your sketch is to have character. Emphasise the waist, the shape of the skirt, the effect of the collar. Then fill in the details of exactly how the garment should be cut, indicating the type of stitching, pleats, darts etc. and the set of the sleeves. Next give details of the trimmings, buttons, belts etc. It is like making a map, giving first the outline and then the final details and information.

A Typical Working Sketch

All working details are added as the garment is cut and made. A sample of the material used is attached to the sketch and any comments necessary on the handling of the fabric and style should be noted at this stage.

Calculating the selling price for the garment

In order to establish the correct selling price for any garment, the manufacturer takes into account the type of woman for whom it is intended and considers the sizes accordingly. If a garment is to be sold in sizes 12 to 20, for example, the basic calculations may be made on size 16. Depending upon the company, the selling price is based upon the original design or sample garment, made in the pattern room.

When studying books on production you will find that this method of calculating price will vary according to the companies. With large mass-production firms the accountant's figures are correct to the last decimal point and time and motion study in the manufacturing of the garments is a fine art.

Costing

(will depend on current prices)		Cost
2.5 metres of woollen material	@ .... per metre	.....
·5 metres of inter-facing	@ .... per metre	.....
2·0 metres of lining	@ .... per metre	.....
Trims (threads, belt, buttons, buttonhole twist)		.....
Overheads (electricity, heating, labour, rent, etc.)		.....
Plus profits (approximately $33\frac{1}{3}\%$)		.....
	Total	

N.B. Usually a sample costing is generous

Requirements of a good working sketch

A good working sketch should have the following:

    Front and back view
    All seam lines carefully marked
    Type of seams indicated
    Direction of pleat
    Buttons and buttonholes indicated
    Indication of the stripe, check or plaid

Give three other details which should be indicated on a working sketch.

Fashion Collections

Clothing trade procedure

When once a design has been worked out the material is chosen. The garment is patterned and cut, modifications being made in this process.

The sample garment is now made, every detail being checked and alterations made where necessary on garment and pattern. If chosen for the collection, the garment is fitted on the model girl. The garment is displayed to all the buyers from the wholesale firms. If it is a great success, it is photographed for newspapers and magazines and for advertising purposes.

Prototypes are made for the agents in different parts of the country or abroad who will each receive a copy of the original garment and show a repeat of the collection in the area where he or she works.

The columns of the fashion magazines or newspapers are scanned for favourable comments to help with sales.

After this the designer is back at work on the next collection. The factory meanwhile is busy ordering large quantities of fabrics to arrive at the right time for the garments to be made and despatched to the buyers.

The timing from design to despatch is very carefully worked out. Otherwise lack of delivery can mean cancellation of orders and loss of business.

Collections for wholesale firms

Although collections of garments from wholesale firms are usually shown in May and November, mid-season showings are often made for the more fashion-conscious buyers. British collections are influenced by Paris and it is usual for designers to attend the couture collections to buy certain 'toiles' and pick up ideas that can be modified, or used as a basis for a number of designs. Many go to get ideas on fabrics, accessories, new lines, new silhouettes, colours, the mood of the moment and possible future trends.

Couture showings

Usually in January and August buyers, fashion editors, designers, etc. converge on Paris for the couture collections. Buyers for wholesale and retail houses are required to purchase a toile or toiles for a fee before receiving a ticket to attend the shows. Toiles that are chosen after the showings indicate new trends and are reckoned suitable for adaptation to ready-to-wear garments. In January, autumn and winter styles are shown, and spring and summer styles are featured in November.

Questions

1   Describe a classical garment.
2   What garments are known as the 'bread and butter lines'? Illustrate two.
3   Illustrate two gimmicky dresses recently in the news.
4   The mood of the moment plays an important part in influencing fashion. Give examples.
5   How long a life span has fashion?
6   Illustrate some 'fads' that have been short-lived (either accessories or actual garments).
7   Sketch and describe three garments from the current collections and show by additional sketches how you would adapt each design for the ready-to-wear market.
8   Design three trouser outfits for medium-price wholesale firms, suggesting materials to be used.
9   Shortening of skirt lengths changes the proportion of the bodice-skirt relationship. Sketch three examples.
10 Suggest three colour schemes which would be suitable for a range of mix-and-match separates in plain and printed jersey. Design a range of separates suitable for this material and for selling in a ready-to-wear store.
11 Show how you would interpret the trend for greater movement in skirts. Illustrate three dress skirts and three suit skirts.
12 Describe and illustrate the differences between
    (a) a working sketch for the pattern maker
    (b) a fashion sketch which may merely give a silhouette.

Wardrobe Planning

Designs for special occasions

Clothes express moods and feelings. Those designed for special occasions tend to restrict the wearer to that special activity or use. Consider first of all what the designs should be suitable for.

The occasion:	Wedding or official function
The climate or season:	Summer or winter
The time of day:	Early morning or evening
The type of client:	Sophisticated or immature
The age group:	Young or middle-aged
The price range:	Expensive or medium-price
The setting:	Town or country
The fashion trend:	Traditional or ultra-modern

List of clothes for special occasions

Casual or sportswear – usually easy-care, comfortable garments, mix-and-matches, blouses, skirts, jeans, sweaters, slacks, often made in washable sun-resistant, rot-proof and durable material.

Active sports – comfortable and casual garments, easy-care materials, freedom of movement required as well as a little glamour.

At home – these can be anything. They can be kinky and trendy or simple and comfortable. Anything you please. If entertaining, they can be formal or casual.

Travel wardrobe – travel washables that do not wrinkle and can be packed easily, e.g., wool, crease-resisting polyester, acrylics, and nylons. Classical styles.

Party clothes – can be most extreme, ultra-feminine, high fashion or casual. Any lengths, although the present mood dictates longer skirts.

Formal wear – long dresses; not strapless, as they would not be suitable for dinner parties; not too bulky for going to theatres and getting in and out of cars.

Business or town wear – this will vary according to the place, the occasion and accepted ideas of what is suitable. Usually darker colourings are better, with light contrasts.

Suits – tweeds make good basic country outfits. The cut, texture and trim will determine the exact category, i.e. business, town or cocktail wear.

Maternity wear – concealment and camouflage are the main aim. Maintaining an attractive appearance is of great importance to the expectant mother and comfort is one of the greatest assets. Separates such as slacks with expandable waistlines and long overblouses, provided they do not contrast too much, can provide a variety of outfits. Dresses are more comfortable than skirts and can be more slimming, especially if interest can be focused on the face by pretty necklines, scarves and collars.

Wardrobe Budgeting

Main items required

Coat – suitable to cover the basic length of dresses (usually 3 cm more) and sufficiently full in the skirt to take bulky garments.

Dress – with little detail so that it can be 'trimmed-up' with a scarf, brooch, flowers or beads. This means that the fabric should have no pattern and be of plain texture and of easy-care or cleanable material. Choose a colour which suits you.

Suit – good, medium colour or light material, depending on the season. Winter – wool, summer – easy-care crimplene, trevira etc.

Hat – depending upon the individual. A hat should be chosen to balance the whole body, so always look in a full length mirror before deciding. Remember that a hat chosen for a wedding would not be suitable for a business outfit.

Shoes, gloves and handbags – buy good quality, but not necessarily to match a coat. You can have a contrast or a colour which blends.

Lingerie

Bras and girdles *must* fit well. Comfort is the primary aim. Do not distort outer garments by squeezing into small-sized girdles and so creating bulges in unsightly places!

The body changes shape as one matures and incorrect fitting can harm the muscle tissues. Girdles and bras must always be carefully selected for fit and comfort and as methods of production become more advanced, it is advisable periodically to compare shapes as fashions change. Top garments are greatly affected by the undergarments and bumps and bulges showing the outlines of undergarments can spoil the appearance of any dress or suit.

Fashion magazines

Studying fashion magazines helps. Try to see copies of the following:

> *Harper's Bazaar, Vogue, Seventeen, Linea Italiana, Elle* and *Women's Wear News*

Keeping up to date

As fashions change, so garments are discarded and replaced. When possible, analyse each item in the wardrobe for its suitability, its comfort, colour and style, whether you like or dislike it and whether repairs are needed.

Exercise

It is said that clothes express moods and feelings. Sketch six garments that obviously show where they are to be worn and when.

When would you use diamante beading and highly coloured trim?

Design six dresses for an outsize person, putting swatches of material with each design.

An extremely tall girl wishes to look shorter. What materials would you use, what colours? Would you proportion the garment differently from the average size?

A thin woman wishes to look fatter in the bust. Design two dresses, stating materials and colours used.

Points to bear in mind

Pinafore dresses – allowing for constant changing of blouses, should be in good easy-care material and interesting textures.

Classical cuts – have the advantage that they can be dramatised by the addition of a strategically placed brooch or trimming.

Two-colour combinations – create a focus of interest.

Pretty necklines and high placed fashion details – can create diversion well away from the stomach.

To help you decide

Ask yourself:
Is the purchase an asset to the wardrobe?
Does it improve my appearance?
Does the colour suit me?
Is it good value for the price?
Is it easy to care for?
Will it mean buying new accessories?
Will it wear well?
Is it fashionable?
Is it comfortable?
Is it suitable for the climate?

Does it fit into my budget?
Am I being influenced by the saleswoman and do I really want it?
Is it suitable for the occasion?
Is it in good taste?

What is good taste?

Good taste means a material in harmony with the style. It means a colour that suits you. It also means a garment appropriate to the place and the circumstances. It means a garment in proportion to your build and character and an expression of you as a person.

Keeping an immaculate wardrobe

Daily care is the secret of an immaculate wardrobe. This involves brushing, airing, pressing, repairing any tears, replacing buttons and removing spots before they set into the fabric. The life of garments can be greatly extended if proper treatment and maintenance is given.

What to do

Always check labels on garments.
Hang garments on well-shaped hangers.
Check labels on garments for ironing instructions.
Treat stains before washing or cleaning.
A disinfectant is sometimes advisable when using a launderette, or at home if there is any risk of infection, as bacteria can survive on clothes.
Clamp skirts and trousers on to snap-type hangers.

Use starches where extra body is required for fabrics.
Every garment should have a dust cover.
Heavy cloth garments should be regularly brushed and aired.
Brush silk with flannel.
Brush velvet with velvet.
Re-press pleats.
Shrink away any bagging in knees of trousers or in the seat of skirts.
Very full skirted dresses have loops in the waist and these should be hung on special hangers.
Boots and shoes should be padded with paper or shoe trees put in the feet to keep them in shape.
Fasten coats, especially double-breasted ones, to prevent creases.
Do not put garments in overcrowded drawers.
Garments with full and puffed sleeves hanging for a long time should have the sleeves stuffed with tissue paper.

What not to do

Do not pack garments too tightly into the wardrobe.
Do not iron without checking the correct temperature.
Do not wash if the label says dry clean.
Check dyes, especially red, before putting into coin-operated cleaners.
Do not leave buttons on garments if there is a possibility that they may disintegrate in cleaning.
Do not iron velvet. Steam instead or use a velvet board.
Do not hang garments cut on the bias on hangers. It may make them stretch out of shape.

PART 2   TEXTILES

Studying Textiles

From earliest times, even in the most primitive cottage, cloths have been woven for home decoration and comfort. Everyone uses textiles, for the clothes one wears, for furnishings in the home and on dozens of occasions in daily life. It is necessary to study textiles to understand why one cloth is more serviceable or durable, cleaner or 'handles' better than another, especially if cloths are to be chosen for particular designs. Materials must be tested to make sure they are suitable for the purpose for which they are going to be used, while care of the fabric must be considered too.

For a designer it is essential to appreciate fabrics and their proper use, to understand fibres and investigate their properties thoroughly and to be familiar with all new finishes and fabric descriptions.

Fabric Construction

Examine a piece of woven fabric and observe that it has interlacing sets of yarn running lengthwise and crosswise. It is from the inter-lacing – or weaving – of these yarns (whether by twisting, overlapping, made parallel or separ-ated) that textile materials are made.

The textile industry uses many different kinds of fibres. Some have been used since the early years of civilisation. Others have become important only in recent years.

Cotton

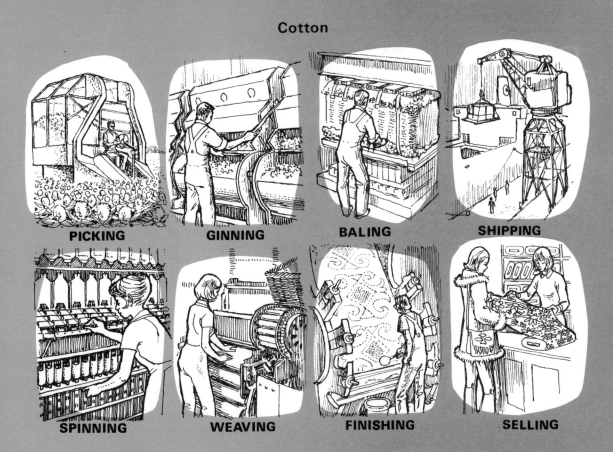

PICKING   GINNING   BALING   SHIPPING

SPINNING   WEAVING   FINISHING   SELLING

Origin

Cotton is grown in warm climates, mainly tropical or sub-tropical. At one time it was called 'tree wool' because it grows on trees and is like the fluff of the black poplar. The cotton boll is picked by hand or machine and taken to a gin to remove the fibres from the seeds. The length of the fibres ranges from 5 mm to 5 cm. The shorter downy fibres are known as cotton linters and are used to produce some types of rayon, e.g. acetate and cuprammonium rayon, while the longest fibres are made into Sea Island cotton.

Characteristics

Cotton ranges from the finest muslin to heavy calico. It washes well, can be boiled, absorbs moisture and allows good ventilation to the skin. It has a fresh and sometimes dull appearance.

Handling

Creases easily and shrinks. Cool to the hand, can be smooth, glossy, napped, light or heavy. An absorbent fabric and easy to wash. Excellent for hot climates and sportswear. Retains whiteness. Blends well with other fibres.

Sewing

Test for shrinkage first. Use hand needles 7 to 11, depending upon weight. Thread 40 to 50, mercerised or satinised cotton. (See chart for machine needles p. 128.)

Pressing

Iron on right side if sheen is required. To achieve good results dampen to iron. Minimum iron to cool iron. (Do *not* iron seersucker.) Test first but usually for cottons without special finishes a hot iron 200° C can be used.

Washing

Whites can be boiled. Coloureds 85° C (very hot), for cotton articles without special finishes where the colours are fast. Most cotton garments, unless otherwise labelled, can be machine-washed. Hand-wash delicate cottons. Cotton lace usually shrinks heavily, so always test first. Fabrics containing a mixture of cotton and synthetic fibre, e.g. acrylic, must be washed at a lower temperature, usually 48° C.

Linen

Origin

Flax, used in the manufacture of linen, is grown in a moist temperate climate and in a loamy soil and is recognised by its clear green stalks and tapering leaves with clouds of pale blue or white flowers. Ireland, France, Belgium, Holland and Russia are flax-growing countries. In early summer, flax is pulled by machine and afterwards it is steeped in water to loosen the fibre from its parent stem. When dry, it is moved to the mill where the stem is removed. This is done by fluted rollers and by revolving blades which beat the stems. After this it is hackled, going through a series of pins graduated in fineness, so that eventually it comes out clean, like beautiful golden hair. In the next process it is given a twist in the roving frame. Before spinning, the yarn is put into a trough of hot water which softens the residual pectic materials. It is then spun on to bobbins like magnified sewing machine bobbins and can be blended with both natural and man-made fibres.

Characteristics

Linen is absorbent and durable. It is stronger wet than dry, washes well but creases badly.

Handling

Cool and pleasant to wear. Easy to handle but creases badly. Frays badly. It has a tendency to shrink so should be checked for shrinkage first. The yarn is irregular, which is part of its beauty, although it can be very smooth and strong. When wet it is even stronger. When blended with other fibres it is less liable to creasing and shrinkage. Some linens can be 'springy'. Linen has different fabric finishes.

Pressing

Use a hot iron setting 200° C. Steam iron can be used, but the right side should be protected from shine by using a damp cloth. For springy type cloth, use a damp cloth on the wrong side and afterwards, if the seams spring up, press them flat with the bare iron.

Sewing

Use mercerised or satinised cotton or silk. Hand needles 8 to 10, depending upon the weight of the linen. Pull thread to straighten ends as linen is difficult to tear.

Washing

Can be boiled and either hand-washed or machine-washed. Untreated fabrics can be bleached and starched. White linen without a special finish can take a very hot (85° C) maximum wash. Fast-coloured linen without a special finish can be washed at 60° C.

Wool

Origin

The sheep are shorn after dipping and sometimes the wool comes out from under the shears (nowadays electrically operated) clean and white. Often, however, it is greasy and so goes through a scouring process. Then it is dried, sprayed with oil and bleached. The wool is dyed in the dye-house either before it is spun, in the yarn or after it has been woven.

Many years ago weaving was done by hand. The first spindle was just a stick with a stone at one end. The thread was prepared by adding bits of fibre. This soft bit of fluff was stretched and twisted into a thread and wound round a spindle.

About five hundred years ago the first spinning wheel was invented and had a treadle so that the wheel could be turned by the foot, while the hands were free to guide the thread. The modern spinning wheel works on that principle.

Chief processes in the manufacture of wool

SORTING
Raw wool

SCOURING
The wool is washed in large tanks to remove grease, dust and dirt

SPINNING
The thick ropes are put into a spinning machine which draws them out, making them longer & thinner. At the same time a twist is given to make the yarn stronger

CARDING
The wool is combed on a machine so that the long fibres form long thick ropes. These are wound into balls called TOPS. They are used for felt & other woollen materials

WEAVING
The yarns are made into fabric by weaving or knitting

DYEING
Dyeing may be carried out at the yarn stage or after weaving

29

Spinning means twisting the yarn and winding it on to bobbins. These bobbins take the place of the old fashioned spindle and they turn so quickly that you can hardly see them move as they fill with finely twisted thread. The thread is then taken away ready to be woven. Basic principles still remain, even though machines driven by electricity are used today. In many parts of the country, cottage craft industries are still in existence and the old fashioned hand looms are used.

Characteristics

Wool is warm and absorbs moisture. It has a soft fuzzy appearance. Worsted, which is produced from the longer fibres, has a tighter twist than wool. Worsteds have a stronger twist than other woollen fabrics and they can be woven with distinctive patterns, chiefly the twill weave. Virgin wool is new wool. Shoddy is made from regenerated wool, such as old woollen garments, picked, pulled and rewoven.

Handling

Warm and elastic, drapes well, is absorbent and is warmer wet than dry. Woollen gabardine, because it has a firm weave, repels water. Woollen cloth has a fuzzy surface, but worsteds have a smooth surface. Wool can be blended with other fibres. Two features of wool are that it shrinks and has an attraction for moths. However, it can be treated to overcome both these disadvantages.

Sewing

Pure silk thread is best for wool, but otherwise use terylene thread which gives with the material. Polyester threads can be used. Use a high number for fine weaves and a lower number for making buttonholes.

Pressing

Press on the wrong side with a damp cloth and warm iron (150° C). A steam iron, pressing lightly, is suitable for georgettes and crêpes, but always use a damp cloth on the wrong side.

Finish with light pressure and a cloth (slightly damp) on the right side. Never place a bare iron directly on to woollen material. Leave to cool slightly before moving, as wool gets very soft when warm. A solution of vinegar and water helps to remove shine.

Washing

Unless labelled washable, it is better to dry clean. Hand-wash sweaters etc. at a temperature of 40° C (warm). Always check for shrinkage first and rinse thoroughly. Some wool mixtures can be machine washable (warm minimum wash 40° C).

Silk

Origin

Silkworms can only thrive in countries where the climate is favourable. The silkworm is like a caterpillar and for commercially produced silk the most important species is known as the *bombyx mori*, commonly called mulberry spinner because its diet consists of the leaves of the mulberry tree. In a life of only four to five weeks, during which a silkworm changes its skin four times, it grows to a size of nearly 8 cm, or thirty times its size at birth. After this the worm spins itself into a tightly fitting cocoon. For this purpose it extrudes two cobweb-like silk threads from spinneret glands in the head. They are coated with gum, and are then merged into one thread. This thread is used to form the cocoon, and can measure as much as 3,000 metres or more. It is from these cocoons that the silk is produced after the silkworm has completed the transformation to the stages of chrysalis and moth and emerged from the cocoon. The cocoons are opened out, degummed, washed and dressed and the fibres are combed and straightened out.

Characteristics

Soft, lustrous, light and warm. Good draping qualities. Spun silk, manufactured by a different treatment of the raw material, has less lustre. Wild silk yarn is irregular.

The Birth of the Cocoon

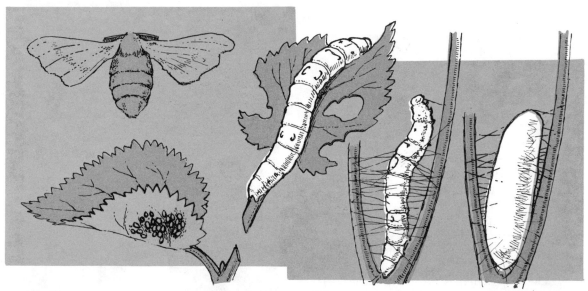

Handling

Soft, smooth and luxurious texture. Slips and marks easily. Drapes well. Can be warm and thick yet not heavy. Can be woven or knitted. Some types of silk resist creasing; others crease easily but can be given a crease-resisting finish. Can be blended with other fibres.

Sewing

Use pure silk thread. If not available, use satinised cotton thread or mercerised. Hand needles, depending upon weight, 9 to 11. (See machine needles chart in 'making up' section, p. 128.) Use fine steel pins and pin in seam allowance.

Pressing

Water marks silk, especially plain weaves. Use a medium hot iron on the wrong side. Pressing on the right side can cause shiny marks. Press seams open carefully. Heavy silks require a damp cloth. Press on the wrong side, then finish on the right side but be careful not to produce a shine on the fabric. Use a warm iron (150° C). Use a damp cloth for cultivated silks. Wild silks need to be dry. If they contain synthetics, iron to the correct temperature for the synthetics.

Washing

Look at the label. Some blends are washable. If unsure, dry clean. Lingerie is usually washable. Protect silk from perspiration. Do not wash silk crêpes.

Man-made fibres

The main classes of man-made fibres

Man-made fibres may be described as those which do not, like wool, cotton, silk or flax, have a natural origin. They are fibres produced entirely by the chemical treatment of certain raw materials, such as wood pulp, petroleum extracts, corn, cotton linters and by-products of coal, and have changed their form (and certain other characteristics) to become long and short fibres.

Acetate	Dicel, Lancofil, Lancola, Lansil, Lo-flam Dicel
Acrylic	Acrilan, Courtelle, Dralon, Dynel, Orlon
Modacrylic	Teklan
Polyamide	Antron, Blue 'C' nylon, Bri-nova, Bri-nylon, Celon, Cumuloft, Enkalon, Enkasheer, Shareen, Tendrelle
Polyester	Crimplene, Dacron, Diolen, Tergal, Terlenka, Terylene, Trevira

Polyolefine	Courlene, Cournova, Ulstron
Polyurethane	
(elastomeric)	Lycra, Spanzelle
Triacetate	Tricel, High-bulk Tricel, Tricelon (filament blend with Celon)
Viscose Rayon	Darelle, Delustra Fibre, Durafil, Evlan, Vincel, Sarille

The manufacture of synthetic yarns and threads

Yarn can be manufactured:

Lustrous or dull
In any length of staple
In any degree of fineness
In any coloured filament or staple by dyeing the spinning solution.
In textured qualities to provide drape, handle, stretching, absorbency and crimping.

The raw materials are treated chemically and sometimes melted by heating to form a viscous liquid which is then extruded through very fine holes in a nozzle called a spinneret. The filaments produced are solidified in various ways. The filaments can be stretched, crimped and cut into whatever lengths are required. Before they are cut, they are called 'continuous filament yarn'.

Drawtwist machinery: nylon yard is cold drawn (stretched) and twisted into textile fibre

Filament and staple

Before 1900 all fibres were natural. Now there are more man-made than natural fibres. The fibre is the basic ingredient of any fabric. The most natural yarns are made from staple fibres. These consist of natural short fibres. (The length is described as 'staple length'.) Silk is the exception, as it is produced in a long, continuous thread called a filament. The two basic forms of textile fibres are:

Filament – a fibre of continuous length, long enough to be used in a fabric without other additional fibres. Silk, for example, contains about two miles (3 km) of continuous twin filaments. Man-made filaments can be several metres long.
Staple – a name given to fibres of limited length. To make a continuous length of yarn, staple fibres have to be twisted together. They range from 5 mm to several

centimetres in length. The shorter fibres cause more surface ends and consequently make a weaker fabric. The longer fibres produce smoother yarns and have less attraction for dirt; consequently these fibres tend to be stronger and more lustrous.

Properties of man-made fibres

Elasticity, fineness, length, strength, cohesiveness, lustre, heat, conductivity, absorbency, cleanliness and washability, affinity for dyes and resistance to mildew.

Advantages of man-made fibres

The properties of a fibre during manufacture can be modified, e.g. elasticity, lustre, colour, size, strength and shape. They can be controlled and adjusted to many types of use and can be produced cheaply enough for the mass market. They can be blended with natural fibres and so can resemble materials made from natural fibres, while giving crease-resistance.

Disadvantages of man-made fibres

Synthetically produced fibres do, however, have some disadvantages. Nylon, for instance, has a tendency to change from white to a yellowish shade in the course of time. Some man-made fibres have a low melting point and excessive heat can shrivel them into holes. Certain synthetic fabrics are uncomfortable to wear in hot weather.

Investigate some man-made fabrics for yourself and find which materials have the following disadvantages:

1   Ready absorption of dirt, making frequent washing necessary
2   Loss of whiteness after washing
3   Distortion of shape after the garment has been worn
4   Threads of the garment easily pulled or 'snagged'
5   Change of colour during ironing
6   Unsuitability for pleating
7   Restriction of the skin's normal breathing
8   Irritation caused to the skin.

Have you observed any other disadvantages? If so, list them and if possible obtain a swatch of the fabrics and keep it for reference.

Acetate

Origin

Acetate, British in origin, was first produced as a continuous filament yarn in 1920. It is a fibre derived from cellulose, its chief raw material being cotton linters (the short unspinnable hairs of the cotton boll) or wood pulp.

Properties

Acetate has a particularly rich and attractive appearance. Age has only a slight effect on its strength and it will give lasting wear if properly cared for.

It has exceptionally good draping qualities.

It has good dyeing and printing properties and will take fast dyes.

It can be spun-dyed to give a high degree of colour fastness (colouring materials are added to the spinning solution before it is extruded).

It has a good natural recovery from creasing.

It has a high resistance to mildew and is not attacked by moths.

It is absorbent.

It is the man-made fibre most closely resembling natural silk.

Acrylic

Origin

Acrylic fibres are true synthetics, being produced mainly from acrylonitrile, a liquid derivative of oil refining and coal carbonisation processes. Acrilan is an American-developed fibre produced in the United Kingdom and Courtelle is an entirely British fibre. Orlon, the first acrylic fibre, was invented by Du Pont in the U.S.A. in 1949.

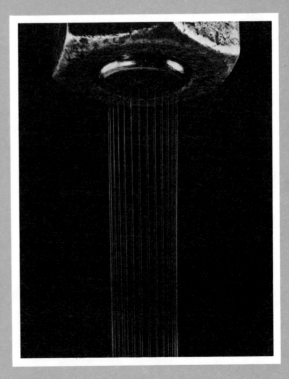

The 'dry' spinning of cellulose acetate yarn by extrusion through a jet assembly

Properties

Acrylic fabric has a warm, soft cashmere-like 'handle' together with lightness in weight.

It is strong and very hard wearing.

It is non-irritant.

It does not shrink or stretch.

It has good crease recovery and resilience.

It has heat-setting properties, e.g. fabrics made from 100% or blends containing 50% or more acrylic fibres can be durably pleated.

It is unaffected by mildew and moths.

Polyamide (nylon)

Origin

Nylon, which belongs to the polyamide group, has been made in Britain since 1941. Nylon is produced entirely from mineral sources. Its raw material is crude oil, from which various organic compounds are obtained, which are chemically treated with reagents to produce nylon polymer.

Properties

Nylon is extremely strong and durable. It maintains its strength when wet and regains it completely when it dries out.

Nylon has elasticity combined with strength and has high shock resistance, useful in industry for ropes and conveyor belting.

It is fatigue resistant.

It has abrasion resistance.

It can be 'heat-set' to a permanent size and shape.

Nylon fabrics are easy to wash and quick to dry and need little or no ironing.

Nylon does not burn and is among the safest of textile fibres.

Nylon is excellent for dyeing.

It is not attacked by moths or mildew.

Crimped nylon yarns can put stretch into swimsuits and stretch trousers; bulked nylon yarns can give warmth and softness to knitwear.

Nylon is produced as staple fibre as well as continuous filament.

Polyester

Origin

Terylene, the world's first polyester fibre, was discovered in 1941 in the research laboratories of The Calico Printers Association Limited and was developed by ICI. It is a synthetic fibre and is made from ethylene glycol (known to motorists as 'anti-freeze') and terephthalic acid which are derived from petroleum. Polyester fibre is now manufactured in a large number of countries and is sold under various trade names.

Properties

Polyester fibre is very strong and has a high resistance to abrasion, making possible the production of sheer, lightweight fabrics with good strength and wearing qualities.

It is equally strong when wet.

It is resilient, giving crease resistance. .

It needs little or no ironing.

It is shrink resistant.

As it resists stretch, it is suitable for sewing thread, and garments made from it keep their shape well.

It has heat-setting properties and fabrics made from 100% polyester fibre or fabrics containing not less than 55% polyester fibre blended with wool or 67% blended with cellulosic fibres can be durably pleated.

It is mothproof and resistant to mildew.

It has resistance to damage by strong sunlight, especially through glass.

In spun form it has great warmth of 'handle'.

In varying degrees it can be mixed and blended with other fabrics.

Polyurethane

Origin

Polyurethane yarns, sometimes described as 'synthetic elastomer fibres' are becoming increasingly important, especially in the manufacture of foundation garments and lingerie. Two types of yarn are now available commercially; monofilament and fused twistless

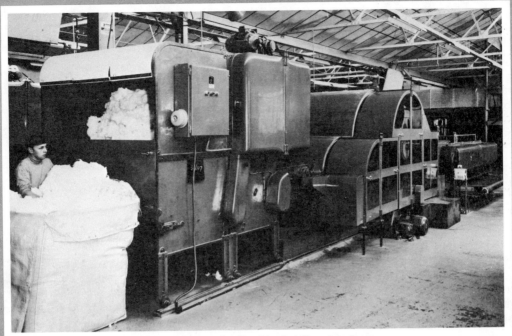

Above: Production of yarn from staple fibre. Feeding blended fibres into hopper

Below: Filaments of viscose rayon yarn leaving the acid bath and joining fibres from other jets in a tow which will form the staple

multifilament. The fabrics marketed under the trade names Lycra and Spanzelle are much used in corsetry, lingerie and swimwear. They give them a lighter and prettier look and more comfort and length of life than was ever possible before.

Properties

These fibres have great elasticity and elastic recovery.

Their power is much greater than that of extruded rubber.

They have high resistance to many chemicals and to perspiration.

They are light and versatile.

Elastomer fibres are always used in conjunction with other fibres and these generally determine the type of washing required. With corsetry and swimwear hand-washing is usually advisable.

Triacetate

Origin

Tricel is the registered trade mark for the triacetate fibre first produced commercially in the 1950's by British Celanese Limited. The primary raw materials from which it is made are wood pulp and petroleum chemicals.

Properties

Tricel is similar in strength and appearance to acetate but is more robust in wash and wear.

It has heat-setting properties and suitably constructed fabrics can be permanently pleated.

It resists creasing.

It has excellent resistance to shrinkage and stretching.

It resists soiling and is easy to wash.

It is quick-drying and suitably constructed and finished fabrics made from 'Tricel' require little or no ironing.

Viscose Rayon

Origin

Viscose rayon, a continuous filament yarn, is a British invention, first produced commercially in 1905. It is a cellulosic fibre, its raw material being wood pulp. It accounts for nearly 50% of the total world production of all man-made fibres, and is the most widely used. This fibre is still undergoing development, despite the length of time it has been in production.

Properties

It is a naturally clean, white fibre.

It has good dyeing properties and will take a wide range of fast colours.

A full range of 'spun dyed' yarns is available to give a high degree of colour fastness particularly for checks, stripes and jacquard designs.

It can be 'easy care' finished to give wash and wear stability.

It is completely mothproof and has a high resistance to mildew.

It has good moisture absorption.

It has non-static properties, significant in linings and hospital uses.

Handling Man-Made Fibres

There are so many new and different fabrics on the market these days that the labels should be read and the instructions carried out before pressing and sewing. Here, however, is a general guide.

	Acetate	Acrylic	Viscose Rayon	Tri-ester
Sewing	Allow extra seam width for fabric that ravels. Use polyester threads or silk, nylon, terylene thread on lustrous fabrics.	Terylene, polyester threads or mercerised cotton.	Sews much like cotton.	Use fine pins and needles. Adjust tensions. Use polyester or mercerised cotton thread.
Washing	Hand-wash, machine-wash or dry clean as the label advises. Wash in warm water. Wash quickly. Avoid wringing. Line dry.	Wash according to instructions. Good washability. Machine or hand-wash. Detergents can be used.	Read label. Dry clean for some; hand-wash or machine-wash for others. Handle carefully when wet, as this fabric can stretch and lose its shape. Can be safely dried in launderette dryer.	Can be washed or dry cleaned. Remove stains instantly. Rapid drying.
Pressing	Use tissue under seam edges to prevent marking right side. Press damp. Press according to label – usually cool iron.	As label, but usually as for rayon setting. Cool iron and press lightly. Do not use steam iron on courtelle jersey or iron when damp.	Follow instructions on label – usually medium iron.	For blends treat as the main fibre. Usually requires little or no ironing.

Relative toughness of fibre

FLAX

Natural

COTTON

Artificial

ACETATE RAYON

VISCOSE RAYON

TERYLENE (H·T)

TERYLENE (M·T)

NYLON (H·T)

SILK

NYLON (M·T)

0   1   2   3   4   5   6   7   8

Project

1 Make a note of new fabrics and their blends. Describe their advantages. Find out what materials have recently been discontinued and why.

2 Collect six samples of cloths and discover their finishes. What fibre does 'Springbak' come from and what finish does it have?

3 Obtain small samples of coloured fabrics and test them for colour fastness. Report the procedure used in your test and also your findings.

4 Here is a list of silk, woollen, linen, cotton and man-made materials all jumbled up. Sort them out under the proper headings: Chambray, Drill, Tailor's canvas, Brushed rayon, Ciré, Terylene, Tulle, Velour, Gabardine, Denim, Bandanna, Peau de soie, Nuns' veiling, Serge, Hopsacking, Cashmere, Felt, Crimplene, Sarille, Velvet, Slipper Satin, Flannel, Broadcloth, Duck, Calico, Winceyette, Piqué.

Testing Fabrics

Linen Squeezing Test

Pull the yarn through two tightly pressed finger tips. If the yarn is linen it emerges straight and stiff. If cotton, it emerges drooping and limp.

Breaking Tests

Recognising the yarn by breaking is one means of identifying the fibres. Take a strand about 30 cm long from the fabric and gently untwist it. Other strands may have been combined in the original spinning operation so untwist carefully until a single strand is obtained. Use a microscope to examine the ends and as you break the yarn apart the various fabrics will be distinguished by the following characteristics:

Cotton: Cotton will snap and show ends that are fuzzy, even, short and brushlike.

Linen: Because linen has long staple yarn, extra length may be necessary and again this must be gently untwisted. Linen has long straight, stiff pointed ends, usually lustrous and uneven at the tips.

Wool: The fuzzy yarn stretches easily because of its elasticity. When broken, the fibre ends are spiral and wavy.

Silk: This again stretches easily when gently pulled and will snap apart at the final stretch. The ends appear lustrous and very fine.

Rayon: Greater tension is needed for this yarn when it is dry, but if moistened it will break more easily. The fibre ends are lustrous and have a stiff brushlike appearance.

The breaking test for spun rayon differs according to the material it simulates. When it simulates linen or cotton the loss of strength when moisture is applied indicates that it is rayon.

Questions

What is the average length of raw silk filament needed from the cocoon of a mulberry silk worm?

What are the irregularities woven into silk fabrics (and known as a characteristic feature) called?

Which country is the world's biggest producer of silk fabric?

What characteristics do the following materials share? – Crêpe-de-chine, Georgette, Ninon, Crepon.

Name a 'silk town' in England.

What is a dupion silk?

Name the three general groups of fibres and their sources.

Name six animals whose hair lends itself to various uses in the textile trade.

How does the length of the staple affect the quality of the fabric?

What quality of acetate would be advisable for winter underwear?

How does a napped surface affect the cleanliness of a garment?

Why is elasticity important in fabrics and textiles?

Weaving Fabrics

The weaving process

If you can imagine a simple loom where the weft thread moves alternately under and over the warp thread, you will have an accurate idea of what happens when yarns are woven into plain weave.

The loom is set up or threaded with the warp threads, which are usually placed closer together at each edge where the weft threads turn round. This forms the selvedge.

The weft threads are woven in and out of the warp by means of a shuttle. Groups of warp threads are lifted up and down by a frame called a 'heddle'.

Pattern is introduced in various ways: (a) different colours (b) different weights of thread, both warp and weft (c) altering the weave.

From these three techniques, the permutations of patterns are endless. Today the basic principles are the same, but a factory loom looks very different from the early hand looms, while sophisticated machines can now produce highly complicated and intricate designs.

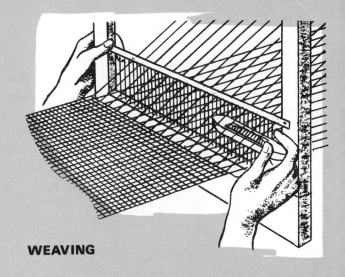

WEAVING

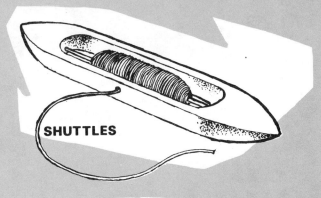

SHUTTLES

A Jacquard loom producing Seraceta Duracol brocade fabric

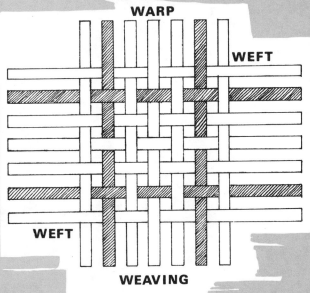

WARP

WEFT

WEFT

WEAVING

Above: A weaver straightening out warp ends
Below: Kirkland circular Jacquard knitting machines with 18 needles per 2·5 cm

Plain Weave

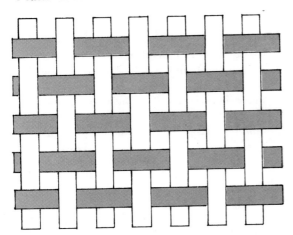

Hopsack Weave

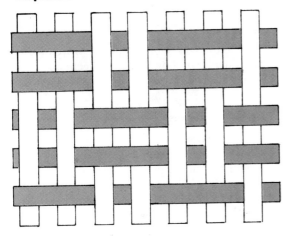

Two and Two Twill Weave

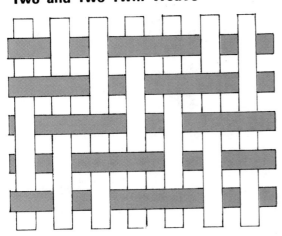

Types of weave

Plain weave is like darning, one up and one down.

Haircord
This is produced by a lengthways rib, alternate rows of one up and two down, two up and two down.

Hopsack or basket weave
Hopsack or basket weave is two up and two down.

Herringbone weave
This produces a zigzag pattern as the number of threads taken up or down will alternate.

Satin weave
As long a warp thread as possible is exposed to give the satin effect.

Twill weave
The weft threads cross the warp threads at different intervals, over one and under three and this produces a diagonal rib.

Damask weave
The damask weave is woven on a Jacquard loom, named after its inventor. This loom is used by most countries in the world for weaving any textile with a pattern. The design is drawn on squared paper to the scale of the loom and the squares are shaded to indicate where the warp or weft threads are to lie underneath and where they are to appear on the surface of the cloth to make a pattern. The lengths of cardboard which are an integral part of a Jacquard loom, are perforated to correspond to the shaded squares.

The weavers prepare the loom by threading the long metal needles of the warp threads, contained in a frame called the harness.

The perforated cards are stitched into a long belt which is hung in loops above the loom. When the loom is in motion they move forward and when the perforations come exactly opposite the needles which control the warp threads, the right threads are automatically lifted, so that the weft threads pass across or under them. That is how intricate design patterns are produced.

Special Fabric finishes

Finishes in materials

Finishes increase the value of the material, give it certain advantages and make it suitable for many different purposes.

The disadvantages of the cloth can also be minimised.

Shrinkage

During the weaving process fibres tend to revert to their natural state, causing shrinkage. By shrinking the fabric in the finishing process, it is possible to reduce subsequent shrinkage to a minimum. Cloth is wetted, allowed to dry without tension and then pressed flat or steamed – or it can be shrunk by a chemical treatment. All these treatments qualify for a 'pre-shrunk' label, but the fabrics are often liable to further shrinkage when washed.

Synthetic resin can be used to prevent fibres from swelling when wet. Many washable dress woollens are now available.

Cotton can be treated for shrinkage, e.g., by tebilizing, Sanforizing or the Grafton anti-shrink process, while the Serono and triple-three processes are used for viscose rayon.

Creasing

You have seen labels 'minimum iron', 'everglaze', 'minicare', and no doubt can remember several others. The fibres most apt to crease badly are cotton and linen but nowadays these are treated with a special synthetic resin so that it penetrates the fibres. It is then baked so that the resin will not dissolve when the garments are washed. Silk and rayon can also be treated, while wool fibres are mixed with synthetic fibres to produce crease-resisting cloths.

Drip-Dry Finishes

Chemical resins are used and the care of drip-dry finishes varies, so read the instructions on the labels. They usually apply to cotton fabrics, although synthetic fibres with blends of natural fibres have drip-dry and shape-retention features.

Staining

Fabrics can be treated with silicones but after several washings the resistance to staining diminishes.

Flammability

Winceyette, cotton, cotton net, linens and rayons are flammable cloths that can be treated so that if in contact with a flame, they only char, and do not flare or blaze. Garments with this treatment should not be bleached, boiled or washed with hard water as a soap deposit will make them flammable. The following materials meet the British Standard requirements for low flammability and are suitable for nightwear: Lo Flam Dicel (acetate) and Teklan (modacrylic).

Protection from Moths and Mildew

Wool, cotton and linen can be protected against mildew. Inorganic salts are used. Cotton fabrics may be proofed at home by soaking the cloth in very soapy water then straightaway dipping it into a solution of copper sulphate.

Waterproofing

To achieve this, cloth is usually woven closely and then treated by wax and silicones. It repels water in showers but not in downpours.

Decorative finishes

Shining material

Cotton can be calendered or polished on one side. This finish can deteriorate with washing. Cotton is also mercerised by being passed through a solution of caustic soda and stretched. Poplin threads are treated this way.

Embossing

A raised pattern is stamped on the fabric and then it is set with resins and heat. Cotton, acetate and triacetate can be treated in this way. Washing will weaken this finish.

Seersucker

This non-iron material is produced by weaving some threads loosely and others tightly. The waffled effect can also be achieved by chemically shrinking stripes of threads after weaving.

Brushing

Cotton, acrilan, viscose rayon and nylon can be brushed to give them a fluffy appearance, although this increases the flammability of the cloth.

Fabric Dyeing and Printing

Imparting Colour

Material can be dyed in the yarn or after it has been woven. Fibres react differently to the same dye. Colours may be affected by light, bleaching, water and washing, perspiration or gas fumes. Colour can be imparted by chemical reaction rather than by absorption. This produces an excellent degree of fastness and can be used on wool, silk, nylon, rayon and cotton. Colour is, to a certain extent, controlled by the British Colour Council in this country.

Removing dyed cloth from a winch dyeing machine

Printing

Roller Printing

The pattern is engraved on a roller, one for each colour and part of the pattern. The fabric passes round a central drum and the rollers pass first through a bath of dye and then press on the fabric, printing a pattern upon it as it rotates.

Block Printing

The design is carved on a wooden block and it is pressed into the dye and then on to the fabric. This is repeated until sufficient fabric has been covered. Very often you will find small inaccuracies in this type of fabric. It is a costly process and very slow.

Screen Printing

Short lengths of cloth are printed and are laid on a long flat table covered with a thick wool felt pad, an oil cloth that protects the wool felt and a cotton cloth to take up colour from the dyed fabric. The screens are made from silk or wire gauze stretched on wooden frames. The background not required is lacquered and the dye is pressed through the unlacquered pattern. Separate screens are required for each colour and beautiful colour effects are produced.

The process can be done by hand or by a machine operated by one man.

Screen printing of acetate woven fabric on an automatic screen printer

43

Tentering

To prevent fabrics going out of shape when the cloth is put on to rollers or boards, they are passed through a tentering machine. Tenterhooks are inserted into the selvedge to bring the material back into shape and are usually inserted into the right side of the cloth. The direction of the holes can be used later as a guide to check the right or wrong side of the fabric.

Examining finished fabric before despatch

Rainwear cloth entering a pin stenter

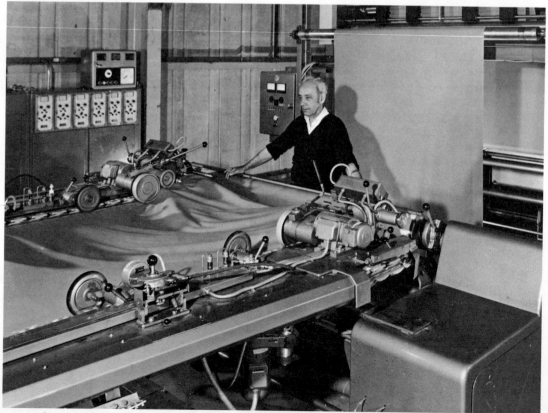

Different Types of Fabrics

Pile fabrics

Pile fabrics are usually warp and weft, but with a third thread introduced which loops all over the right side.

Velvet

Velvet is produced as pile but the loops are cut, as also happens with plush or mock suede.

Foam-backed

Polyurethane foam can be used to back many fabrics. It is stuck to the top fabric with an adhesive but can be washed and dry cleaned. It is light, adds body and insulates.

Two-faced fabrics

Two-faced fabrics have a double right side. This is achieved either by having the wrong sides adhering or by holding them with a fine random thread.

Lace and embroidered net

Many types of lace are produced. Suiting laces are made of heavier yarn, with very little background net but most lace is now machine made. The 'Leavers' method is widely used, whereby two sets of thread are hung vertically while a third set is carried on bobbins. The swinging and twisting of these three sets of threads to a pattern produces the required lace. Chantilly is one of the laces made by this method. Lace used as trimmings can be produced by knitting. Embroidered net is made with a heavier thread on the net in contrasting colours.

For guipure lace, motifs and bars are worked on to a woven fabric such as acetate and it is dissolved away after the lace is completed, leaving the motifs and bars intact.

Knitted fabrics

Imagine hand knitting, with rows of loops interlocking with the rows above and below, so that a tube of fabric like a leg of a sock results. Exactly the same principle applies in machine knitting. Tube knitting, however, can sometimes pull out of shape and so needs to be restored to its correct shape before use.

Bonded fabrics

These have no warp or weft, so they can be cut in any direction. They are made from fibres which build up to a desired thickness and with steam and pressure are matted together. Felt is produced in this way. It does not fray, but it is not strong and has no elasticity. The best felt is made from wool, but it can be made from many other fibres also.

Bonded interfacings

As with bonded fibres, these can be cut in any direction. Fibres are permanently bonded together with a chemical adhesive. They can be made with adhesive on one side or on both sides which enables them to be ironed on to fabric. Paper fabric is also made in this way. Another use for bonding is as a fusible fleece on a paper backing. Fabrics stuck on to a backing material, e.g., jersey, nylon, lace, rayon, etc. are known as 'bonded fabrics'.

Questions

Explain the importance of dyeing from the consumer's point of view.

Why is salt often put into a dye bath?

Why is tie-dyeing expensive?

What fabrics need to be colour-fast to washing, light and perspiration?

Why are most fabrics roller-printed or machine-printed?

Project

Find six materials which:
(a) feel rough and stiff
(b) feel soft and clinging
(c) look and feel shiny and smooth
(d) look and feel transparent and soft
(e) look and feel dull and firm
(f) feel brittle and hard

Name all these materials and describe their constituents. Say whether they are vegetable, mineral or man-made.

Describe how velvet is made.

Describe how pile fabrics are made.

Leather and Imitation Leather

Leather – Different Types

Cabretta	Soft with a glossy finish on the open side.
Chamois	Flesh side of the skin of a small animal (mainly goat) oil tanned (split).
Full grain	Natural surface grain, not treated embossed or sueded.
Glazed	Highly polished outer surface. Sometimes waxed.

Imitation Leathers

Knit back	Plastic surface film fused on to a knitted backing. Flexible and soft.
Vinyl	Plastic film used to coat different fabrics to imitate leather. Texture varies but usually stiffer.
Ciré	A fabric made to imitate leather. Highly polished, either woven or knitted. Textured by heat to resemble leather.
Imitation suede	Flat fabric coated by glue and flocking or by dusting short fibres over the surface.
Embossed leather	A leather-like grain raised and pressed on to a plastic surface.

Leather and Imitation Leather Glossary

Split leather	A skin split to form two layers of leather.
Suede	Soft unglazed leather. Originally kid skin, but nowadays sheepskins are dyed and finished on the flesh side by using a dry emery wheel. Other methods are used, but this is the simplest and the oldest.
Hide	A tanned animal skin approximately 8 metres.
Kid	A tanned animal skin approximately 5·8 metres.
Scabbling	Uneven dyeing producing a shaded effect.
Shaved	Thinned leather producing a uniform thickness.
Side	Half the animal. There are two parts – back and belly – usually cut along the backbone.
Skin	Less than five metres. Taken from the whole animal.
Skiver	The cut edge of leather thinned.
Tanning	Vegetable or mineral substances used to prepare animal skins.

Removal of stains from fabrics

Act quickly before the stain dries. Cold clean water can keep the stain moist while you are deciding on the best solution to use.

Useful solvents
Ammonia – may bleach slightly.
Amylacetate (banana oil) – test first. Very flammable.
Carbon tetrachloride – harmless to most fabrics.
Methylated spirits – test first. Inflammable and can affect some dyes.
Glycerine – useful for fruit stains.
Vinegar – useful for taking away shine.
Warm soapy water.

Absorbents
Salt – must be washed out afterwards.
Fuller's earth – is brushed out when dry.
French chalk – is brushed out when dry.
Blotting paper.
Test first on a hidden part of the garment. Place cotton wool underneath and working from the right side, using a circular movement, work from the outside in. Renew the underpad when it is soiled. After removing the stain, wash or clean. Advise the dry cleaners of any treatment you have given if dry cleaning is required.

If you do not know what has caused the stain, you can experiment cautiously as follows. If the material is washable try cold water, then if that has no effect try warm water. The next stage – and this applies to non-washable fabrics – is to try a grease-solvent such as carbon tetrachloride.

STAIN REMOVAL GUIDE

Adhesive tape
> Sponge with amylacetate or a dry cleaner. Launder afterwards.

Alcoholic drinks
> Sponge with cold water. Apply vinegar water, i.e. one pint of vinegar to one pint of methylated spirits.

Blood, meat juices, egg, perspiration
> Soak in cold water. If the stain persists, soak in lukewarm ammonia (three tablespoons to one litre of water) or hydrogen peroxide.

Butter
> Ordinary washing. For non-washables use dry cleaning fluid.

Cocoa or coffee and fruit juices
> Dab with a solution of one part glycerine and two parts water, and leave for several minutes. The stain should then wash out. For fruit juices, try water first.

Candlewax
> Rub with an ice-cube and scrape off excess wax with blunt knife. Place the stained section between blotting paper or brown paper and press with an iron.

Chewing gum
> Treat as for candlewax but if the stain persists, sponge with dry cleaning fluid. Launder in warm water.

Grass
> Use methylated spirits as for ballpoint ink, or test with hydrogen peroxide to bleach.

Hair lacquer
> Apply amylacetate and wash afterwards.

Ink
> Soak the stained part in a saucer of milk and test with water afterwards for washable ink. For ballpoint rub with petroleum jelly (vaseline). Sponge with dry cleaning solvent. If it persists treat with acetone (but not on acetate fabrics) or nail varnish remover.

Lipstick or rouge
> Use a proprietary cleaner. If ineffective, try eucalyptus to dissolve the stain. The resulting oil stain can later be removed by carbon tetrachloride or by soap and water.

Mildew
> Mildew is a fungus, and difficult to remove. It grows in warm, damp conditions. Wash in hot detergent solution. Moisten with lemon juice and salt and dry in the sun. If it is an old stain, bleach with hydrogen peroxide. Rinse well.

Tar
> Dissolve with paraffin or special proprietary tar-removers.

PART 3 PATTERN CUTTING

Basic Principles of Pattern Cutting

What is a block pattern?

Having acquired the art of designing simple garments, you now need to know how to put your ideas into a practical form. To be able to make patterns for your designs and to become a good pattern cutter, you need to have a block pattern or master block. This is your first basic requirement.

In pattern cutting a block pattern is a skeleton shape made to a set of measures either (a) to fit an individual or (b) to conform with the specifications required for an average figure in the wholesale trade. A block pattern, when made up, should fit neatly over the body – like a second skin, except for the fact that tolerances on the pattern are allowed for all the movements of the body. Darts are positioned where needed to ensure unrestricted movement and to allow for the flexibility of the body. The darts can be placed anywhere around the apex of the bulge to give freedom of movement and comfort in the garment.

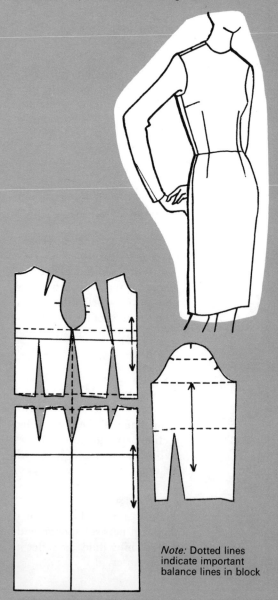

The block pattern consists of back and front bodice, back and front skirt and sleeve – five sections in all. The master template is usually made without seam allowances and hem turnings. The sections of the patterns are plain and only have basic darts.

Many firms will remake their block patterns each season and, to ensure speed and accuracy, often add on the allocated seam and hem allowances.

To economise on time and labour a large number of firms make block patterns of simple styles and sections of garments, e.g. flared and circle skirts, slacks, shirtwaister sleeves, collars, lingerie etc. These are used very often in a season with different cloths and styles. In other words, they are *basic shapes*, to be used again and again.

Note: Dotted lines indicate important balance lines in block

48

Manipulating the darts

How to manipulate the darts to create different styles
This is done by moving the darts into any position around the point of a bulge. Here you have the basic principle of cutting a flat pattern to fit a three-dimensional figure. It is an art requiring common sense, a keen eye for detail, good line and proportion.

Darts can be put wherever you wish, provided the 'apex' or point of the dart is always on the fullest part of the bulge. A dart, therefore, is part of a circle and the widest end of the dart is usually on one of the seams. Darts appear larger when they are longer, even when the angle of the wedge is the same.

You will learn more about dart manipulation later, but first copy out the miniature patterns so that you can gain practice and do the exercises in the following pages.

Retaining the basic block foundation lines

However many times a pattern is cut about for tucks, pleats, godets, yokes or any kind of fullness, the newly designed garment will only fit correctly when the foundation lines of a pattern are as the original block pattern.

Naturally, there are exceptions to the rule – e.g., flares on skirts, sleeves and necklines – and allowance must be made for the type of material used. But as a general rule the basic measurements must be retained.

2 Dotted line indicates movement from basic block to create new dart position

1 Basic block

3 New dart position achieved

A design when finished should conform with the basic measurements of the block pattern

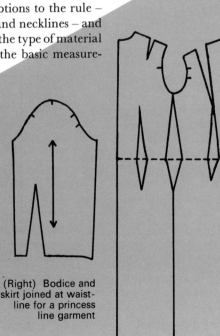

(Right) Bodice and skirt joined at waist-line for a princess line garment

Be practical

Whatever idea you have will be of no value unless the design can be made up in a way suitable for production.

It is no use designing complicated styles unless they are capable of being cut out and made up. This applies both to the wholesale trade and to individual garments.

Questions

1 What would you say was wrong with this sketch?
2 Re-sketch the style as you feel it should be for production purposes.

Cultivate speed and accuracy

Time is a most important factor in the clothing industry, especially in high fashion. As soon as any idea is shown to the public and it appeals, then no time must be lost in seeing that it is manufactured and put into circulation. At the same time one must be absolutely accurate about every section of the pattern, otherwise it will not fit correctly or appear balanced.

Consider the fabrics

Handling the fabrics before cutting the pattern will give you an indication of the best way of cutting. Seaming and the tolerance allowance will depend upon the type of cloth used.

Adjusting the block

It is usual in manufacturing establishments to check the basic block every season and adjust it to the fashion trend, as, for example, when a fashion like the mini skirt comes in.

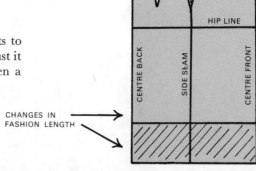

Questions

1 Apart from skirt length alterations, what other alterations have been necessary to a basic block in the last ten years?
2 Do you think the waistline has altered recently?
3 As you look through illustrations of fashion trends, what has altered most through the generations? Is it the length or the waist?
4 Do you think the shoulders of today are too sloping?

Designing by draping

Creating garments on a dress stand

Many designers, although experienced and skilled people, are unable to express themselves sufficiently clearly in sketch form but are able to create wonderfully interesting garments on the dress stand. Often they use a cheap material similar in texture to the proposed cloth, but if possible they use the original material.

After completing the draping on the dress form, they carefully mark all seams and grain lines. The garment is then taken off the 'stand' and laid flat on the cutting table. Pattern paper is laid under the flattened cloth and all the marks for the darts, tucks, pleats or folds are carefully traced through on to the pattern paper. The grain is essential and must be carefully checked, while balance marks on seams are necessary for easy production.

Draping for mass production

For intricate drapes it is as well to keep a calico replica of the basic block to lay against any newly modelled garments. The darts should be closed and the block laid against the garment when it is on the stand and the seams and size should be checked carefully. The seams can be marked on a dress form by narrow tape, so that the work of checking can be simplified.

Producing a pattern by flat pattern cutting

Advantages
1 Much quicker for large-scale production.
2 Economical.
3 Accurate.
4 Any size can be made.
5 Makes pleats or tucks more accurate.
6 Quantity of material quickly calculated.

Producing a pattern by modelling

Advantages
1 Better when draped effects are required.
2 Effect of the line can be seen immediately.
3 Material faults can be corrected at the beginning.
4 A better perspective can be achieved.
5 The texture of the cloth can immediately be seen and whether or not it is suitable for the style.

Combine both methods – Either method when carried out accurately will be successful for producing a pattern, but, as you can imagine, for modern methods flat pattern cutting with a combination of modelling is essential. Knowledge of both aspects of pattern cutting will enable you to acquire the art of true perspective. It is not easy to draw a good line on the flat for collars or necklines without seeing them on the stand or person. If the paper is pinned on the stand you immediately get a true perspective and can rectify accordingly before the pattern is cut in the cloth. If striped materials are used the pattern can be marked to give an indication of stripes, angles, or plaid effects and, if necessary, adjusted at this early stage. Also it is important to observe the rules of proportion. This skill can be developed by observation and experience, by making sure the lines are in harmony with the rest of the pattern.

Various Pattern Cutting Tools

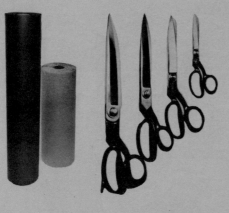

Interleaving
tissue

Scissors

Plain white
marking paper

Stanley
knife

Tape
measures

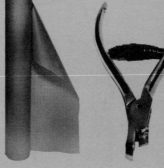

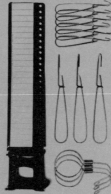

Aluminium
rules

Spot and cross
marking paper

Pattern
notcher

Heat-Seal
marking paper

Sartorac
pattern hooks

Carbon
paper

Underlay
paper

Pattern
punch

Edge-
Lok

Anti-Fusion
paper

Lay
powder

Tailor's
chalk

Pattern cutters' equipment

Write out a list of all the tools shown in the illustration which would be used for home dressmaking and state their purpose.

Write a list of the items used in wholesale pattern cutting and find out their particular uses.

Tools required

You do not need *all* these items, but it is as well to know the tools that are used. All you need for your present requirements are the following:

1   A good-sized table with a plain smooth surface for cutting.
2   Several lead and coloured pencils with sharp points.
3   A pencil sharpener.
4   Several sheets of plain white paper or brown paper.
5   A good *straight* ruler, preferably plastic or steel, as wood sometimes warps.
6   A set square. Again, a good-sized one for full-scale work but a small one will be adequate for the one-fifth scale.
7   A rubber – a soft one that does not tear the paper or leave marks.
8   A tracing wheel.
9   A pair of good-sized shears. Small ones will be suitable for one-fifth scale but not for full-scale work.
10   A bodkin or pattern awl for making holes to denote the end of the dart.
11   Notchers. (Scissors will be adequate until you are experienced.)
12   A Stanley knife, when you are experienced.
13   Drawing pins.
14   Sellotape.

Learning to cut patterns

You have become familiar with the requirements of a pattern cutter, the tools needed and the equipment used in a pattern cutting room of a manufacturing firm. Now you need to know how to cut the patterns. Your next step is learning how to measure a person.

In designing you saw the positioning of the darts; now you should acquire the art of knowing exactly where those darts should be placed when making your pattern. This is where you need to be observant and accurate.

What to do

First memorise these technical terms and abbreviations relating to pattern cutting and measuring:

Bk.	Back
B.	Bust
B. Pt.	Bust point
C.	Centre
C.F.	Centre front
L.	Line
G.	Girth
H.	Horizontal
Nape of neck	Base of neck
Tolerance	Ease of movement
Nk. Pt.	Neck point
Nk.	Neck
Shl.	Shoulder
Shl. Pt.	Shoulder point
S.S.	Side seam
U/A.	Underarm
V.	Vertical
Scye	Armhole
Draft	Plan of the style
Meas.	Measurements
Increments –	Amounts added to or deducted from one size to another

Taking Measurements

Learning to take personal measurements

Before you start make sure you have the following:

1 Tape measure (not old and tatty but clean and strong).
2 Piece of elastic (narrow to tie around the waist and over the bust).
3 A box of pins.
4 Pencil and paper.

Make sure the person to be measured is standing normally, and if she is to have a full-length dress ask her to remove her shoes or to tell you the height of heels of the shoes she is likely to wear for the occasion. It is always advisable to find out if she will be wearing the same foundation garments for the fitting, as they can affect the finished garment tremendously.

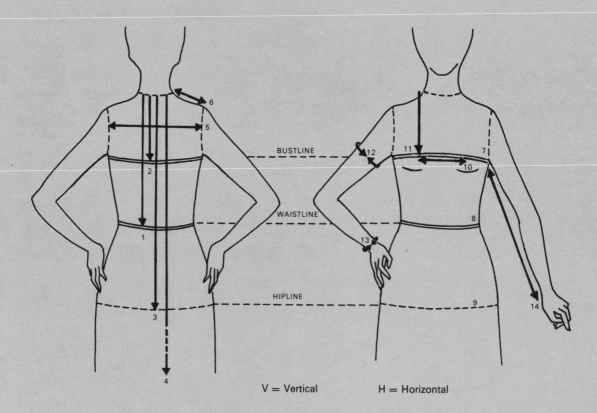

V = Vertical   H = Horizontal

Measure in this order: Use the piece of elastic to tie under the arms (not to be uncomfortable, but in the normal armhole position) for the depth of scye and for deciding the position of the waistline.

1 V. Nape to waist (tie elastic around the waist).
2 V. Nape to depth of scye (tie under arms but not too high).
3 V. Nape to largest part of hips.
4 V. Nape to length.

5 H. Across back.
6 H. Across shoulder from neck point.
7 H. Bust.
8 H. Waistline.
9 H. Hips.
10 H. Bust point to bust point.
11 V. Neck point to bust point.
12 H. Arm girth.
13 H. Wrist.
14 V. Underarm.

54

Measurement sequence for skirts:

1 Waistline to length required
2 Waistline to largest part of hips (If the person tends to be curvaceous take two hip measurements)
3 Round waistline
4 Round hipline

Size 12 measurements

	Body Measurements cm	Plus Tolerance	Final Measurements	Increments
Nape to waist	40	—	40	·6
Nape to depth of scye	22	—	22	·3
Across back (half)	17	1	18	·6
Width of neck (half)	7	—	7	·2
Shoulder	12·5	·5	13	·2
Bust	88	8	96	4
Waist	64	4	68	4
Hips	92	4	96	4
Upper arm girth	27	6	33	1·3
Underarm sleeve length	41·5	2·5	44	·2
Wrist	17	3	20	·5
Bust point width	8·5	—	8·5	·2
Bust point length from neck point	24	—	24	·2
Crown height	—	—	14	

Completing the size chart

Sizes	8	10	12	14	16	18	Increments
Nape to waist	38·8	39·4	40	?	41·2	41·8	·6
Nape to depth of scye	?	21·7	22	22·3	?	22·9	·3
Across back (half)	?	16·4	18	17·6	?	18·8	·6

To enable you to become conversant with measurement charts (this is so important when measuring people and gives you an indication of the proportions of the figure) complete a size chart for sizes 8, 10, 14, 16 and 18.

Size charts

Body measurements:
Without tolerance or 'room for movement'.

Size	8	10	12	14	16	18
Bust	80	84	88	92	96	100
Waist	56	60	64	68	72	76
Hips	84	88	92	96	100	104

Finished measurement:
Extra ease or tolerance is allowed over and above the body measurements so that a person can move and breathe easily, without any restriction from the garment.

Size	8	10	12	14	16	18
Bust (8 cm)	88	92	96	100	104	108
Waist (4 cm)	60	64	68	72	76	80
Hips (4 cm)	88	92	96	100	104	108

Standard measurements or proportionate measurements

These are sets of measurements used in the wholesale clothing trade to enable the general public to buy their correct size of garment. Each size is given a numerical designation (10, 12, 14, 16, 18, etc.) The body measurements of the sizes have been scaled to conform as nearly as possible with the dimensions of our neighbours on the Continent, although measurements vary between countries and firms. Dress stands are constructed to the standard measurements, so that the garments can be checked and fitted on the stand.

Individual measurements or direct measurements

These are measurements taken for an individual, so that a garment is specifically made to the measurements taken and should conform to the shape and size of that person (or the dress stand).

Preliminaries

Before making a block, practise measuring people of all types and all shapes, until you can use the tape measure with skill and confidence. Cultivate the habit of observing the figure you are measuring by looking for such features as prominent hip muscles, shoulder blades, muscu-

lar forearms or a thin or thick neck. If possible, make notes about these details and try to retain a picture of the figure in your mind as you make the pattern. Do not accept other people's measurements as accurate. Since everyone takes measurements in a different way, the tape measure risks being either too slack or too tight.

It is also necessary for you to observe where the shapings on the figure are to be placed on the pattern; you can then position the darts where required.

A pattern cutter should know how to make a master pattern for individuals or for standard measurements. In the following pages the system given for making a block has been made as simple as possible, but it must be emphasised that the success of the pattern will depend on correct measurements and shapings.

Advice

When making a block pattern for the first time, make it in one-fifth scale. This will enable you to get a general idea of the procedure so that later you will make it in full scale quite quickly and easily. Each time you make a block try to cut down your time by a certain amount. In this way you will become speedy and proficient.

Use the reference numbers on the illustrations to help fix in your mind the best order of working when you are drafting the pattern.

SIZE CHARTS: Remember that these will vary from country to country. While the sizing system 12, 14, 16, etc. for women's garments remains in use in Britain, actual measurements are now given in centimetres and inches. Thus dresses, suits, jackets and coats are measured in 4 cm intervals up to size 14 and 5 cm intervals after that, e.g. Size 16: Hips 102 cm/40 in, Bust 97 cm/38 in. Bear in mind also that tolerance allowed over and above the body measurements will vary according to the material and design. For a firm medium woven cloth the tolerance allowance is 8 cm. For a finer or softer weave it could be 4 cm and for a fine jersey even less.

Cutting a block pattern

What to do

Have all the measurements in the right sequence so that all you need to do is look down your list and measure accordingly. Here is the method – but you must realise that the first time you make a block you will think it is difficult, the second time it will be much easier, while the 'penny will drop' at the third attempt and you will discover that it is fun and quite quick to make a pattern to individual measurements. As with everything else in life, practice makes perfect.

As the skirt is the most simple garment to make, start with this, taking the measurements in the right order and try to complete in one-fifth scale first.

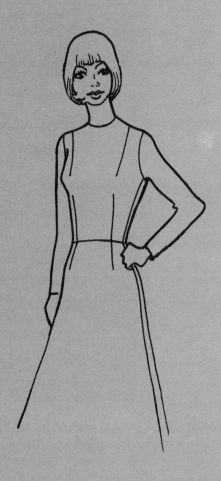

The basic block diagrams in the pages that follow have been drawn to one-fifth scale.

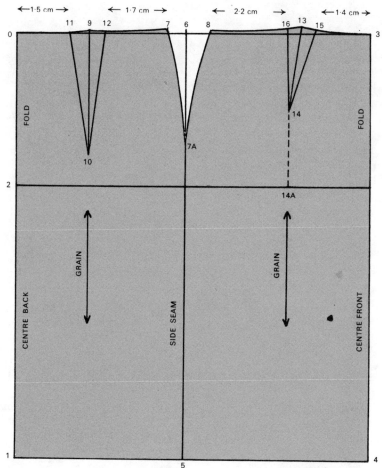

		One-fifth scale	Full scale
Commence the construction by drawing a line for the centre back skirt to correspond with the desired length of the garment		9·6	48 cm
		11·2	56
Back skirt			
0–1	Skirt length	11·2	56
0–2	Hip length	4	20
0–3	Waistline	9·6	48
3–4	Centre front	11·2	56
1–5	Side seam	4·6	23
	Draw line upwards to intersect 0 line		
0–6	Raise above waist	·1	·5
6–7		·5	2·5
6–8		·5	2·5
Shape side seam 7–7A–8 8–7A		3	15
0–9	Centre of back dart	2	10
	and raise above waist	·06	·3
9–10	Parallel to centre back, measured from 0 line	3·2	16
9–11	and 9–12	·5	2·5
	Draw lines to complete dart		

Make smooth line from 0–11–9–12–7. This completes the back skirt. The amount raised above the waistline would be the same for sizes 8–18. (Standard measurements only.)

58

Front skirt

3–13	Centre of front dart	1·8	9
	and raise above waist	·2	1
From centre front along hipline measure to 14A		2·2	11
Raise for apex of dart at 14		2	10
Join 13–14			
13–15 and 13–16			
Draw lines to complete dart			
15–14 and 16–14 should be the same length.		·4	2
Make smooth line from 8–13–3			

Repeat the procedure in full scale and trace the back skirt on to firm paper adding 2·5 mm for side seam and 1·5 mm for waistline. Indicate grain line and hipline on pattern and fold the dart towards the centre back so that it runs flush with the waist seam. Lay the back side seam against the front side seam and check that the hipline and hip curve correspond before finalising on the front pattern. Repeat the addition of waist seam allowances and fold the front dart towards the centre front.

The skirt block is now completed

Making the Bodice Block

As you embark on the block, first remind yourself that you are making a plan of the body, as an architect makes a plan of a house. Draw all your skeleton lines in first and then with careful attention to the curves and the shaping, draw in the neckline and armhole and so evolve your shape before you determine the position for the darts. Be accurate and square correctly, because if you do not do this right at the beginning all your points will be slightly off balance.

Start at the centre back and work towards the centre front, making all lines 48 cm.

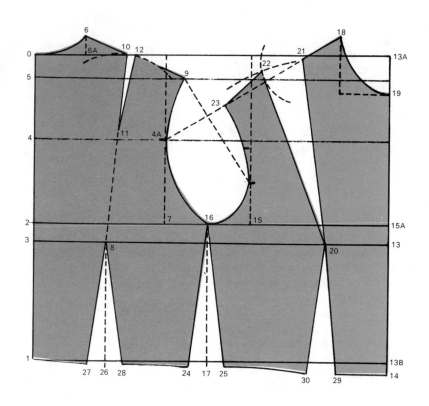

		One-fifth scale	Full scale
0–1	Nape of neck to waist	8	40
0–13A		9·6	48
1–13B		9·6	48
0–2	Depth of underarm	4·4	22
0–3	Bust line	4·9	24·5
0–4	Across back	2·2	11
0–5	Shoulder point line for all sizes	·6	3
0–6A	Back neck width (half)	1·4	7
0–6	Raise vertical and draw curved line to 0	·5	2·5
2–7	Across back; square to 0 line	3·6	18
3–8	Apex of waist dart	2	10
6–10	Shoulder dart Draw line to 8	1·2	6
10–11	Shoulder dart length	2	10
11–12	Swing an arc same measurement as 11–10		
10–12	Measure allowance for width of dart	·2	1
9–12	Draw line to finalise shoulder	1·4	7
3–13	Half bust plus tolerance	9·6	48
13B–14	Draw a vertical line to join 13A–13B and lower centre front waist to 14	·3	1·5

Note: The measurements 0–2 to 0–5 are bracketed with the instruction "Draw in horizontal lines parallel to 0–13A".

15A–15 Front scye line
For all sizes divide the bust by 5,
then minus ·5 (full scale) ·1 (one-fifth scale)   **3·74**   **18·7**
Draw line upwards to intersect 0. line
15–16 Side seam; half of 15–7.
16–17 Draw a vertical line downwards.
and extend below waistline   **·1**   **·5**

Now you have the framework for the final details. Check that every line is squared before proceeding and curve of back neck is as in the diagram and draw in the armhole curve to the side seam.

13A–18 Front neck width
(back neck measurement minus ·2 (full scale)
·04 (one-fifth scale))   **1·36**   **6·8**
Raise for front neck point   **·5**   **2·5**
18–19 Centre front neck. Square from 18–19   **1·5**   **7·5**
13–20 Bust point   **1·7**   **8·5**
18–4A Draw dotted line to back sleeve pitch
18–21 On dotted line measure from 18 the same
amount as 6 to 10   **1·2**   **6**
20–21 Join these two points (bust dart position)
21–22 Bust dart width: **1·1**   **5·5**
Swing an arc this measurement from 21
20–22 Swing an arc from 20, same measurement as
21–20, intersecting arc from 21
22–23 Same measurement as 9–12   **1·4**   **7**
Join 23–16 making a smooth curve as illustrated, touching the front armhole line
above 15.   **1**   **5**

Side seam:

24–17–25 Either side of 17 measure   **·5**   **2·5**
Join these points to 16 to make the front and
back side seams.
1–26 Centre of back dart   **2**   **10**
Drop below waistline   **·08**   **4**
27–26–28 Measure either side of 26   **·5**   **2·5**
Join 27–8–28 (back dart).
Join 1–27 and 28–24, making good smooth lines.
14–29 Level with 14   **1·4**   **7**
Join 29–20.
29–30 Front waist dart   **·8**   **4**
Join 20–30.
29–20 and 20–30 should be same length.
Join 25–30, making good smooth line.

Measure and calculate the curves in the diagram and keep the shapings in your mind as you fill in the lines for the block. This is most important for the fitting of the sleeve head into the armhole of the bodice. Make a good curved shape for the neckline.

Front sleeve pitch above 15   **1·1**   **5·5**
Front sleeve pitch (2nd) above 15   **2**   **10**
Draw dotted line from 9 to 1st sleeve pitch above 15.

Making the sleeve block

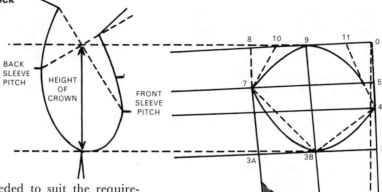

Sleeve styles are needed to suit the requirements of the constantly changing silhouette and the sleeve block is checked every season, modernised and adapted to the fashion trends.

Taking sleeve measurements
If the arm is thin, 5 cm or more would be allowed over and above the basic measurement to maintain the correct relationship between arm girth and elbow. When taking measurements for coats allow extra ease to let the sleeve fit comfortably over another garment.

Height of sleeve crown
Unitl you are experienced, take the height of the sleeve crown from the proportionate measurements. For an approximate measurement it is possible to measure the circumference of the arm scye and divide by three.

The sleeve block

	Finished Measurements	
Proportionate measurements	One-fifth scale	Full scale
Crown height or head of sleeve	2·8	14
Upper arm girth	6·6	33
Underarm length	8·8	44
Wrist girth	4	20

V. Vertical. H. Horizontal.

Proceed to make the sleeve in the same way that you made the skirt and bodice, making first the skeleton shape and then filling in the final details. Leave a space of 10 cm from the top of your paper and 20 cm from the right and left hand sides, before drawing your main line. (One-fifth scale 2 cm and 4 cm.)

The foundation lines of the sleeve

		One-fifth scale	Full scale
0–1	V. underarm sleeve length plus crown height	11·6	58
1–2	V. Forward tilt for sleeve	·5	2·5
	The following lines will be squared from 0–2 and will measure	5·5	27·5
0	H. Square for top of crown.		
0	H. Square for wrist line.		
·3	H. Square for upper arm girth.		
3–4	H. Square for front sleeve pitch	1·1	5·5
4–5	H. Square for back sleeve pitch	·7	3·5
3–6	H. Square for elbow line halfway between 3–2 (approximately)	4·4	22

Constructing the crown

		One-fifth scale	Full scale
5–7	Half upper arm girth. Back sleeve pitch	3·3	16·5
7–8	Raise to intersect 0 line. For centre of sleeve mark point halfway between 0–8.		
8–9	and plus 1 mm (5 mm full scale)	1·76	8·75
8–10	and 0–11 (guiding lines for sleeve crown). Join 10–7 and 11–4. Join 7 to 6, at 90 degree angle, making	·7	3·5
6–12	half elbow measurement	2·9	14·5

Join 12 to 2 at 90 degree angle, making 2–13 half of wrist girth. Halve the measurement 3–3A and draw a line through this point 3B upwards to intersect 0 line at 9 and downwards to waistline at 14. This is the centre of the sleeve.

3B–14   is the underarm seam of the sleeve.

As a guide, draw lines from 7 to 3B to 4 and then make your shapings for the crown as illustrated. The straight lines will help you to calculate the amount to curve inwards or outwards, but make them smooth.

Fold the sleeve on the line 4–2 and then towards the line 9–3B–14.

Trace from 4–3B, from 3B–14, then centre line to 14–2 at wristline.

Fold the sleeve on the line 7–12 and then towards the line 9–3B–14.

Trace as for front (7–3B–14–13–12).

Fold back to make the full sleeve, as diagram on next page. Either cut net or add turnings.

This completes your basic block patterns and now you can, with patience and initiative, make any pattern you wish.

Provision for the elbow

This can be: 1 Eased, 2 Darted, 3 Gathered or made as a decorative feature.

A correctly cut and set-in sleeve should have no folds under the arms or drawn appearance around the upper arm girth. The sleeve should be comfortable and easy and the inside seam should be in line with the thumb.

Practice in block making

When you have completed the block in one-fifth scale repeat it in full scale. Practise making a block to your own measurements. Practise making a block to a friend's measurements. By the time you have completed all these blocks you should be conversant with the procedure and have thoroughly grasped the art of block making.

Notches in bodice and sleeve patterns

So that the sleeve is placed into the bodice correctly, corresponding notches are made in both bodice and sleeve to enable the machinist to match the sections quickly and efficiently.

Owing to the curvature of the armhole, the top edge of the sleeve will not fit smoothly unless extra length is allowed, therefore, the measurements around the sleeve must be greater than the armhole of the bodice, and usually notches are positioned to accommodate the quantity and area of easing. The easing can vary and depends upon the material, the upper arm girth and the prominence of the front shoulder bone. Lack of easing would give the appearance of the bodice eased on to the sleeve. The centre shoulder notch can be adjusted to rectify any fitting or style feature, but the balance of the sleeve must always be preserved.

Assembling notches and marks

Balance marks are given to show exactly where one point should match another on the different pattern sections. Sometimes holes and cross marks are given to show the end of a dart or the position of a seamline or soft fold. Slots are made in patterns for marking seams when top stitching is required, for buttonholes, pockets etc. For wholesale work, separate templates are made. Notches help the dressmaker assemble the garment easily and also show the amount of turnings allowed.

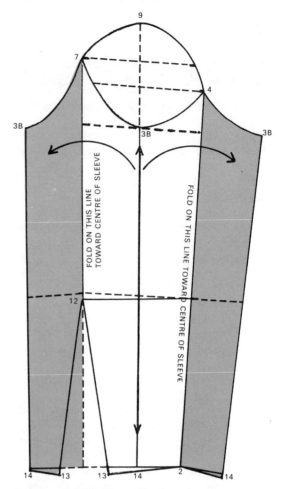

Seam and hem allowance

Each firm decides the seam allowance it will give in its garments. This will naturally vary according to the production and you will find larger seams are allowed on the side-seams and hems for more expensive garments than for cheaper wear. On average, most people use ·5 mm seam turnings for curved necklines and facings and naturally allow more on side seams, e.g. 2 cm. The different firms all have their own standard seam allowances. When seams are neatened a greater seam allowance is necessary. Seams and hems will alter according to the style and the material used, e.g. chiffon material would differ greatly from jersey material.

Certain set measurements must be laid down for seams and it is not wise to have too many different widths of seam, as that could be confusing to a worker.

Dart Manipulation to Create Styling in Skirts

Moving the darts

There are two ways of manipulating the darts:

1   By the slashing method, which is quite accurate provided you cut on the lines.

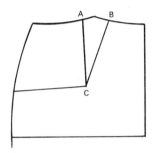

(i) Trace Basic Block on to paper. Indicate position for transferred dart by a line drawn to apex of original dart position (C). Slash exactly on this line to C.

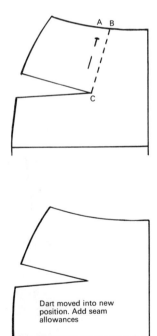

(ii) Fold dart along AC line. Bring AC to lie along BC line, closing original dart and opening dart allowance into new dart position.

2   By pivoting. It is better to use this method when you understand the dart manipulation process, but if you feel like 'having a go' do so. Some people may even find it easier and quicker.

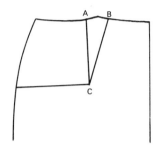

(i) Trace Basic Block on to paper. Indicate position for transferred dart by a line drawn to apex of original dart position (C). Slash exactly on this line to C.

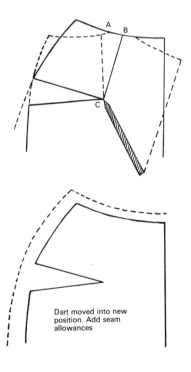

Dart moved into new position. Add seam allowances

(ii) Swing A to meet B. This closes original dart and opens dart allowance into new dart position.

As you learned in the design section, darts are required to produce a good fit and are the excess pieces of material taken into wedges to make a flat piece of material fit the contours of the body. These darts must not change the fit or size of the original darts on the block but they can be put wherever you wish, provided that the apex or point of the dart is always on the point of the bulge.

The wide end of a dart is usually on one of the seams and a dart can be arranged in any position radiating from the point of a bulge.

To transfer a dart into a seam, use the same method as for transferring a dart into a new position, but mark the entire seam line through the apex of the dart, then close the dart by either method on the previous page, but:

(i) Indicate seam line position.
Close dart, creating a bulge in the paper.
Slash one side of seam line to apex of dart.
   Finally, cut the two sections of pattern apart along the remainder of the drawn seam line.

(i)

SEAM LINE

(ii) Slash both sides of the seam to the apex of the dart (taking care that *all* sections of the block remain joined at the apex of the dart) if the dart allowance is to be distributed into both sides of the seam. Make a smooth line.

(ii)

   Finally, cut the two sections of the pattern apart at the apex of the closed dart, and add seam allowances.

Making different skirt patterns

Usually the centre front and the centre back are placed to the fold of the paper; it is then certain that the two sides are identical (unless you are cutting an asymmetrical style).

However, you *can* make a pattern to centre front and centre back only, provided you always indicate whether it is to a seam or fold. A full pattern is generally used in industry, but a half pattern is often used when cutting on the double.

NOTE: Throughout the following diagrams, the dotted lines indicate the position of the Basic Block before adaptation.

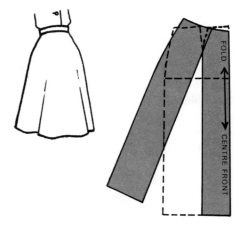

Making a flared skirt
1 Trace block.
2 Close dart.
3 Slash to apex of dart and lay flat.
4 Trace on to new piece of paper after repeating the procedure with the back block.
5 Add seam allowances and keep this as your basic flared skirt block.

Adding extra flare into the skirt
1 Trace the basic flared skirt block on to new paper.
2 Draw lines where extra flare is required and slash on these lines, from hem to waist.
3 Open required amount.
4 Trace new shape on to fresh paper. Add seam allowances and hem.

Graduated pleated skirt

Pleats can be pressed or caught at waist and left as soft folds.

Using flared skirt block (one-fifth scale)

1 Decide the number of pleats required (3) and divide waistline into this amount.
2 Divide the hemline into same number of sections.
3 Draw lines from waist to hem and number sections.
4 Slash and open sections ·5 cm at waist and 2 cm at hemline.
5 Lay sections on a new piece of paper and trace new pattern.
6 Fold pleats into position. Add seam allowances and hem and cut flush with waistline and hemline.
7 Notch and indicate on pattern the grain line and the direction of the pleats.

Note:

Extra can be added for each pleat and seam lines can be made behind pleats.

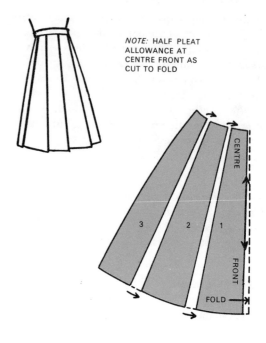

NOTE: HALF PLEAT ALLOWANCE AT CENTRE FRONT AS CUT TO FOLD

Making straight pleats

1 Decide number of pleats and type of pleat (knife, inverted or box).
2 Mark position of pleats on straight skirt block.
3 Reposition darts, distributing half dart into a pleat and remainder in new position above hip muscle.
4 Draw lines from waist to hem and number sections.
5 Lay on new paper and slash where pleats are required.
6 Open sections the required width of pleats.
7 Add extra for centre front pleat (inverted).
8 Add seams and hemline, indicate grain and direction of pleats and notch for easy assembly of the garment.

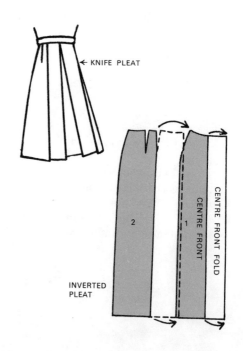

KNIFE PLEAT

INVERTED PLEAT

Gored skirts, sometimes called panelled skirts

These can be cut either from the basic flared block or the straight skirt, depending upon whether the flare is required from the waistline or the hipline.

It is important to remember that the grain is usually placed in the centre of each gore, to allow the flare to be evenly distributed at the hemline. Be sparing with notches. Do not place notches closely together, especially if the material frays. Indicate the hipline as a balance line and if many gores are cut, number each one. Position notches for easy assembly of the garment. For eight or more gores allow extra on the hipline for the thickness of the material used.

Gored skirt from flared block

1 Front and back can be marked separately if desired. Indicate hipline.
2 Divide waistline and hemline into equal sections.
3 Join lines from waist to hem.

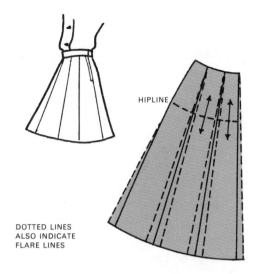

HIPLINE

DOTTED LINES
ALSO INDICATE
FLARE LINES

4 On each side of lines at hem indicate required flare.
5 Join lines from waist to hem.
6 Number sections and indicate grain.

Gored skirt from straight skirt block

1 Trace back and front blocks, laying side seams together and indicate the hipline.
2 On the hipline divide the back and then front skirt into equal parts.
3 Square these points to the waist and hemline and number each section from front to back.
4 Divide the back dart evenly and put in seam lines. Do the same with the front.
5 At the hemline on each side of the drawn lines indicate the extra amount required for the flare. For an average simple flared skirt allow 3 cm (full scale) 0·6 cm (one-fifth scale).
6 Just above the hipline graduate the lines to hemline.
7 Trace out individual sections on to new piece of paper, adding seams and hem. Indicate notches to check balance of skirt.

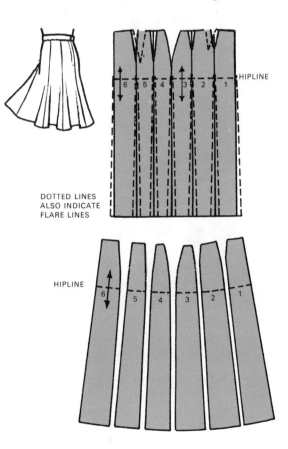

HIPLINE

DOTTED LINES
ALSO INDICATE
FLARE LINES

HIPLINE

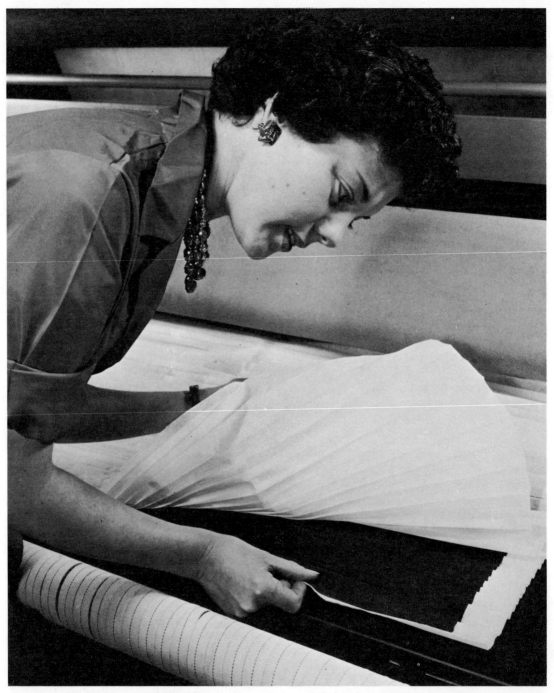

Machine pleating Tricel lock-knit. The fabric, protected by tissue paper, is folded and hot pressed at about 60 pleats per minute.

Pleating and pleating specialists

There are several kinds of pleat – accordion, box, inverted, knife, sunray, vandyke – but the most commonly used are the knife, box and inverted pleats. Seams are usually put behind the pleats and the darts can be divided equally between the pleats, or the shapings can be taken into the pleat itself.

70

Pleated Tricel fabric being loaded into autoclave for thermosetting

Accordion, sunray, vandyke, crystal pleating and combinations of pleating are steampressed by specialists who supply their own patterns. These firms usually require the hems to be done first. If skirts are cut for sunray or accordion pleats, they are usually cut from quarter-circle patterns, where a pattern can be made by drawing two arcs from a central point, one for the waistline and one for the hemline.

Making straight knife, inverted and box pleated skirts
The usual allowance for a pleat is twice the size of the pleat, in addition to the space taken up by it, e.g. a 96 cm hipline skirt with 3 cm pleats would require three times the hip measurement. Pleats can be made according to the style and can be shallow or wide to produce the desired effect. So that bulk is kept to a minimum at the waistline it is not advisable to overlap the pleats unless thin material is used. The waist suppression can be taken behind the pleats. This means that the difference between the waist and the hip measurement can be distributed where necessary. Always place the basic pattern on top of the garment *after* the pleats have been folded in, to check the waist and hip measurements.

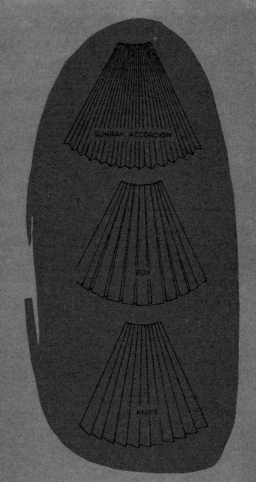

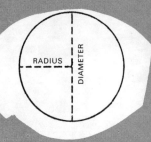

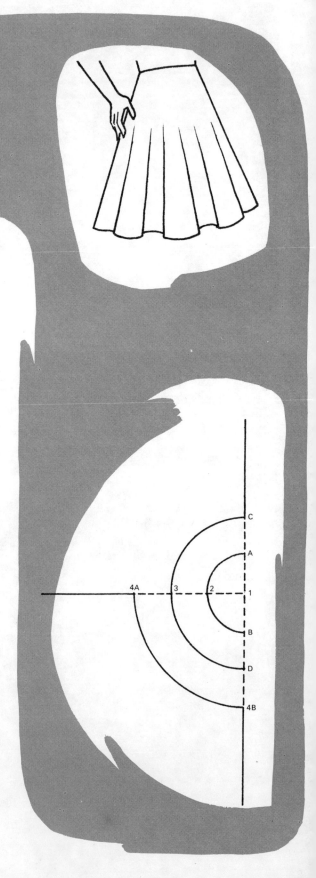

Finding the radius of a circle

To find the radius of a waistline divide by $3\frac{1}{7}$. This gives a half-circle skirt. (Halve this measurement for a full-circle skirt and double the measurement for a quarter-circle skirt.)

This provides an approximate measurement when sending skirts to be pleated. Enclose a piece of material for experimentation, as the heat and steam have varying effects on cloths. It is not easy to level the hems of quarter-circle skirts and where the hems must be machined before being pleated it is advisable to hang the skirt for twenty-four hours. The hem can then be levelled and the pattern adjusted.

Draft for circle, half-circle and quarter-circle skirts

Full-circle	Radius	1–2
	Diameter	A–B
Half-circle	Radius	1–3
	Diameter	C–D

Continue radius and diameter lines to required length, measuring from arc for waistline. Join these lengths with a second arc from 1.

Quarter-circle	Radius	1–4A
		1–4B

Continue radius lines 4A and 4B to required length, measuring from arc for waistline. Join these lengths with a second arc from 1.

As an alternative to cutting two arcs for the waistline and the hemline of these skirts, the block pattern for the flared skirt can be used by slashing and opening out the slashes until a quarter- or half-circle is achieved. It is usual for the centre front and the centre back to be laid to a fold (depending upon the type of skirt). The flare is distributed better this way, as people's waistlines are not circles.

Various skirts

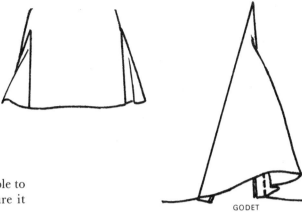

GODET

Skirt with godet

If a godet is inserted into a slit it is advisable to cut it 8 cm longer than the slit and secure it firmly at the top.

A godet can be a triangular section or quarter of a circle.

A goupel pleat is a section added on to a panelled skirt and can be pleated or left to hang in soft folds. The adjoining panel is cut normally as for a gored skirt. The amount added will vary according to the material and design.

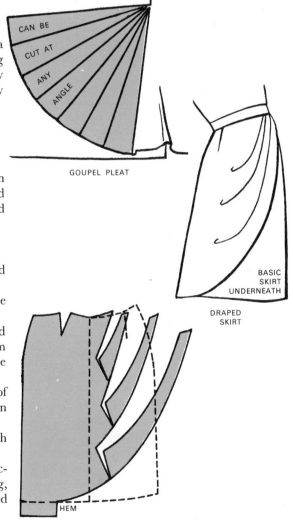

CAN BE CUT AT ANY ANGLE

GOUPEL PLEAT

BASIC SKIRT UNDERNEATH

DRAPED SKIRT

HEM

Draped skirts

It is advisable to make the basic block pattern up in calico to lay over the finished draped skirt so that you can check side seams and waistline.

Method

1 Trace two basic block full front skirts and add seams.
2 On the topmost pattern indicate where folds are required.
3 Close the dart, slash on the fold lines and open slashes as desired, slitting them slightly as indicated, for the pattern to lie completely flat.
4 Lay the slashed pattern on a new piece of paper and indicate position and direction of folds.
5 Pin the folded pleats flat and cut flush with the waistline.
6 While pinned, trace round the curved section and make a pattern for the facing, cutting this to where the hem is 'stepped out'.

Questions

Write a list of figure faults.

What is meant by direct measurements?

What is meant by proportionate measurements?

What is meant by fixed proportions?

What would be the average measurements for a size 12: (a) Body measurements (b) Finished measurements?

What is tolerance?

What is an increment?

Is a template a block pattern?

What do you understand by the word 'draft' in relation to pattern making?

Where is the neck point on the body?

Is it necessary to measure the bust point? If so, why?

Draw a body back view and front view and indicate where you would measure.

List the various measurements necessary to establish a good block pattern.

Do you think it is necessary to take measurements in a certain order?

What individual characteristics of the figure should be looked for when measuring?

What precautions should be taken when measuring?

What means other than flaring can be used to produce fullness at the hemline of a skirt?

Can a dart be in any position around the point of a bulge?

What means, other than darts, can you use to create shapings for a figure?

What is the scye?

What is the first important principle to be learned in pattern cutting?

What is the exception to this principle?

What is the procedure for measuring a figure?

Dart manipulation in bodices

Visualise the style as you manipulate the darts. Look at fashion drawings and try to work out where the basic darts were originally. Darts can be made decorative by adding stitching, pipings, braids, contrast insertions or lace or by machining them on the right side. They can be curved or straight.   When the pattern is completed, darts should not be taken directly to the centre of the bulge. This would decrease the allowance for the bust, especially as it is curved and does not go to a point. Depending upon the bust, the distance from the centre of the bulge will vary, but it is usual to make it approximately 4 cm for a 96 cm bust.

Creating style lines

Darts can be arranged at any angle, they can be divided and fullness can be added to produce soft folds; they can also be transferred into seams.

To create new style lines in bodices, apply the same methods for transferring darts as previously explained for skirts.

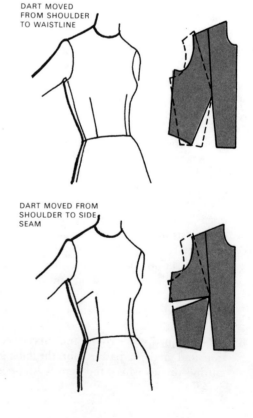

DART MOVED FROM SHOULDER TO WAISTLINE

DART MOVED FROM SHOULDER TO SIDE SEAM

74

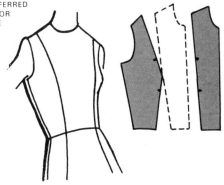

DARTS TRANSFERRED
INTO SEAMS FOR
PRINCESS LINE

Make a smooth curve for the bust. Do not leave as a point. Remember, the body is made up of curves.

DARTS TRANSFERRED
INTO CENTRE FRONT GATHERS

When gathers are substituted for darts, notches should be given for the beginning and the ending of the gathering.

DART MOVED FROM
WAISTLINE TO SHOULDER

The back bodice
It is not advisable to move the shoulder dart to the waist (unless a special design decrees this). Otherwise there will be too much suppression in the waistline. Usually the back shoulder dart is moved into the neckline, shoulder or armhole.

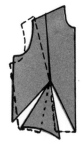

DARTS TRANSFERRED
INTO SEAMS FOR
DECORATIVE EFFECT

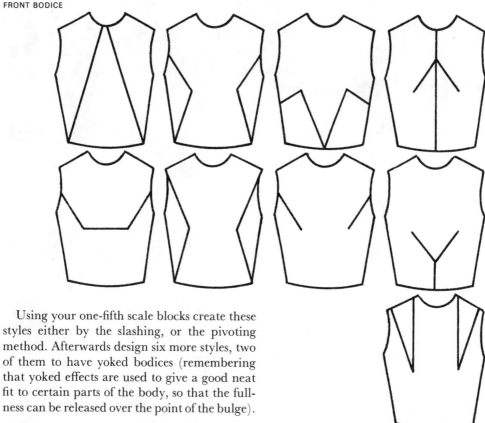

Using your one-fifth scale blocks create these styles either by the slashing, or the pivoting method. Afterwards design six more styles, two of them to have yoked bodices (remembering that yoked effects are used to give a good neat fit to certain parts of the body, so that the fullness can be released over the point of the bulge).

BACK BODICE

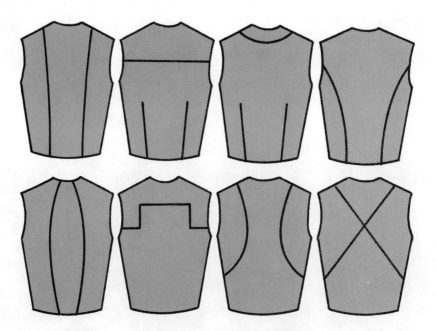

Draped or cowl necklines

Cowls can be cut high or low on the neckline. The principle involved is the same as in cutting a flare, when slashing where the folds are required. There are cowl collars, cowls set into yokes and cowl sleeves. The draping and effect is improved if the material is cut on the bias grain, but in many soft jerseys it is possible for them to be cut on the straight grain. If a bodice is cut completely on the bias a lining is attached to the main body to keep the folds in position. The lining is cut on the normal grain and the folds are lightly caught with a loose catch stitch to hold them in position. With all materials the catch stitch must not be obvious.

Method

1 Decide whether the neckline is high, medium or low cowl.
2 Define the neckline, either to neck point or centre shoulder.
3 Put the shoulder dart into neckline and waist dart into junction of waist and seam.
4 Slash where drape is required.
5 Open slashes the required amount and lay on new paper.
6 Re-define centre front and neckline and fold back facing.
7 Add seams. Put centre front on bias grain.

If a very pronounced drape is required and yet a good fit over the diaphragm is wanted, then the centre front can be shaped and have a seam.

With some soft materials, and depending on the style, the dart can be added to the neckline.

DART MOVED FROM
WAIST TO SIDE SEAM

HIGH COWL

MEDIUM COWL

LOW COWL

Draped effects

Extra fullness is added by slashing the pattern in the direction in which the folds are required and opening out the slashes for the desired amounts. Slash wherever the folds are required, whether vertical or horizontal, and open out, refolding the new pattern and indicating which way the folds are to lie before cutting flush with the seam.

Draped bodice

Method

1 Cut two full front block patterns with the darts in the waistline.
2 On the uppermost pattern, draw the asymmetrical line AB. Trace uppermost front. Cut to shape.
3 Close waist darts and position the lines for the soft folds.
4 Slash and open the required amount suitable for the cloth.
5 Trace the second pattern on to new paper, add facing and indicate direction of folds.
6 Add seams, fold the soft pleats and cut flush with side seam. Indicate grain line.
7 For the other side of the pattern, if desired, leave as block front or cut along CD neckline, depending on whether a high or low neck is required.

Points to note on double-breasted bodices

To emphasise and flatter the bust, the dart can be moved to the junction of the side seam and the waistline. To obtain a good fit define the neckline to come a little below the bust. Do not sew buttons on the bust point and give careful thought to the positioning of the button-holes. If a high-necked double-breasted effect is desired, position the buttons down from the neckline at a distance equal to the button diameter. Do not let the waistline buttons conflict with belts.

Double-breasted bodice

Method

1 Cut two separate front bodices extending 8 cm over the centre front line.
2 Lay centre front line to centre front line and define neckline and extension for double breasted closing.

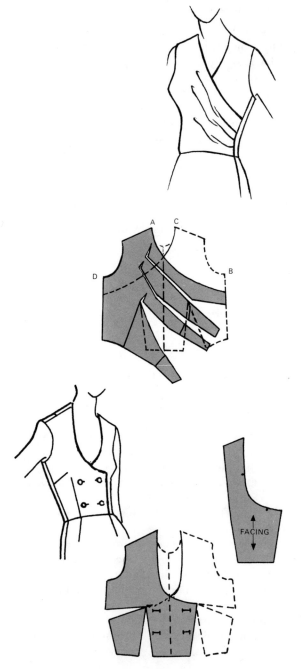

3 Indicate buttonholes measuring either side of centre front.
4 Cut facings to shape as shown.
5 Add seam allowances and for a low necked double-breasted bodice, stay neck edge with tape to prevent stretching.

Sleeves

The balance of the sleeve

A sleeve that is correctly balanced should have the straight grain running vertically down the centre of the arm while the cross grain should run horizontally across the top of the arm. Most sleeves need to hang slightly forward, especially in tailored jackets and coats and the sleeve and bodice pitches should match. When a sleeve is patterned it is balanced to fit into the armhole and the back balance marks are generally put at a point where the across back line meets the crown of the sleeve. In tailoring this would be termed the back sleeve pitch. The front sleeve pitch is usually found approximately 2·5 cm above the base of the front armhole. In between these two points a notch is normally given to act as a guide for a machinist to match the shoulder seam with a notch, usually on the highest point of the sleeve. This, however, can vary according to the position of the shoulder seams. If any other notch is made it is usually given to regulate the fullness required in the head of the sleeve. Every sleeve must have a certain amount of easing to allow for the roundness of the top arm muscle. If fullness is not allowed, it can restrict the arm and create a tightness and also give an appearance of the bodice armhole having been eased into the sleeve head. Naturally, the easing allowed in the head of the sleeve depends upon the styling and the material. A square shoulder effect would require more fullness, whereas a sloping shoulder would not need so much. There are many types of sleeve and some of the basic ones are given here. Using ingenuity and cleverness, many variations can be made and a good pattern cutter will experiment and try out novel styles.

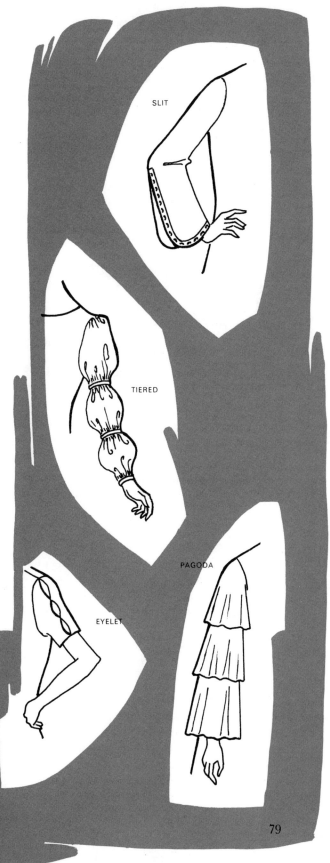

SLIT

TIERED

PAGODA

EYELET

FRILLED

79

Various sleeves

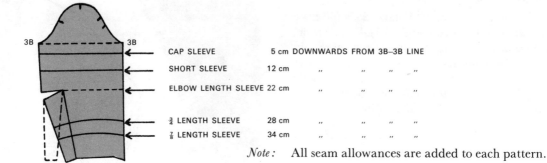

CAP SLEEVE	5 cm	DOWNWARDS FROM 3B–3B LINE			
SHORT SLEEVE	12 cm	,,	,,	,,	,,
ELBOW LENGTH SLEEVE	22 cm	,,	,,	,,	,,
¾ LENGTH SLEEVE	28 cm	,,	,,	,,	,,
⅞ LENGTH SLEEVE	34 cm	,,	,,	,,	,,

Note: All seam allowances are added to each pattern.

Shirt sleeve or active sleeve
This is a casual sleeve and used a great deal in sportswear. The extra underarm sleeve length allows for movement of the arm without pulling too much from the waistline.

Method
The crown of the sleeve is made shorter, by pivoting from the front and back notches.

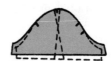

A small amount of easing can be eradicated from the crown if the fabric is a hard material.

Sleeve with darted top
These were fashionable in the 1930's and again, with shoulder pads, in the 1940's. The darts in the crown varied greatly in length and puffiness.

Method
Trace block and indicate the position of the darts.

Slash from the top of the crown and then to underarm.

Slash on the dart lines and open the slashes the amounts needed in each dart.

Draw darts, making the lengths and spacings of equal amounts.

Trace and cut on new paper.

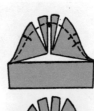

Various types of puff sleeves

There are three principal types of puff sleeves where the puff can be accentuated or merely blended into a particular area:

1 Puff or fullness at the lower edge of the sleeve.

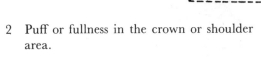

2 Puff or fullness in the crown or shoulder area.

3 Puff or fullness in both the crown and lower edge of the sleeve.

Method

Once the length is established decide upon the type of puff. Indicate and trace the length required from the block on another piece of paper. Slash and open for the amount of extra fullness required

    Slash from the lower edge to the crown.

    Slash from the crown to the lower edge.

    Slash vertically and number the sections.

    Retrace the sleeves on new pieces of paper, indicating the grain lines and applying the notches for the required amount of gathering.

Note: Where a sleeve band is added (Illustration 3), make to fit comfortably so that there is no restriction on the arm muscle when the elbow is bent.

Novelty puff or variation of a puffed sleeve

This is a sleeve where the cuff or lower band is cut as part of the sleeve itself, and the fullness is confined to a certain area.

Method

Mark the width of the band and its position (and extend it beyond the centre line if a lapped opening is required). Trace the sleeve block. Mark the band line, according to the width you want, and also the lines above the band on which to slash for fullness. Open the slashes as much as you need and then trace round the new outlines on to fresh paper. Indi-

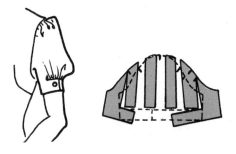

cate by notching the pattern where the fullness will be regulated. Mark the grain line. The cuff section can have a facing or can be grown-on.

Draped sleeves or cowl sleeves

The materials used for this type of sleeve must be soft and pliable and hold the folds in position. Sometimes net or organdie is used as a lining.

Method

Define the length of the sleeve, then trace around the block and cut out the sleeve.

Slash the sleeve as indicated in the diagram, open out the slashes the required amount and then lay on a new piece of paper, allowing a good-sized facing for the top of the sleeve. Surplus fullness can be put into the folds. Notches must be given for easy assembly and the grain of the sleeve must be on the bias.

Lapped or petal sleeve

This pretty novelty sleeve is best with soft lightweight material. It is usual for it to be lined, with a self colour or contrast lining, and the lower edge finished before insertion into the armhole.

Method

Trace the basic block and draw the design lines or petal shapes overlapping the shoulder section.

On new paper, trace first the front portion and then the back and indicate the notches. Cut out and lay the two sections together, eliminating the underarm seam. Position the grain on the previous underarm sleeve seam. When inserting the sleeve, lap the front section exactly over the back, matching the centre shoulder notch.

Flared sleeve

Soft pliable materials are needed for these sleeves. They can be any length and lined if desired. A good curve should be retained at the lower edge to ensure that the flare hangs evenly. The same principle that you learned for cutting skirts applies to sleeves.

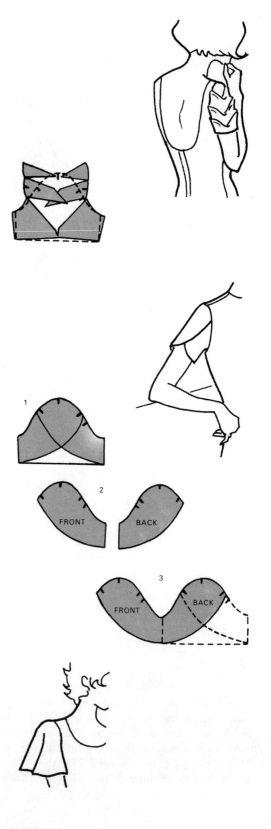

Method

Slash where the flare is wanted – usually from lower edge to crown – and spread the slashes as necessary. If less easing is required in the crown the slashes can be overlapped *slightly*. Trace the new outline on a fresh piece of paper, and indicate the grain. Fullness should not normally be extended on the underarm seam, otherwise the blousing will be pronounced in that position.

Bell sleeve

This type of sleeve flares out evenly like a bell, being much wider at the wrist line than at the arm girth. The crown usually remains the same as in the basic block. The whole sleeve hangs free but the width at the lower edge can vary.

Method

Trace out the basic sleeve block.

Slash to the crown base.

Cut to front and back underarm seams.

Open and spread the slashed sections to the required amount.

Curve underarm seam.

Re-define wrist line and add extra length for turn-up or cut a shaped facing.

Indicate the notches and grain line on the new pattern.

Bishop sleeve

This is a long full sleeve which blouses over a narrow wrist band. It has a clerical origin. The fullest part of the blousing falls away from the body in line with the little finger. The amount of blousing should be more at the side back than the front, to give a more effective silhouette. If the width is increased, the length should also increase and the amount desired to fall over the wrist band should be doubled when making the pattern. Do not put all the width on the underarm seam only.

Method

Mark the slashes after tracing the basic block on a new piece of paper.

Open out the slashes the desired amount.

Re-define the wrist line and indicate the position of the opening.

Cut a narrow band to tie if required (on the fold), indicate the grain and notch the area where the fullness should be confined.

If a great amount of width is required it is better to slash the sleeve evenly in several places.

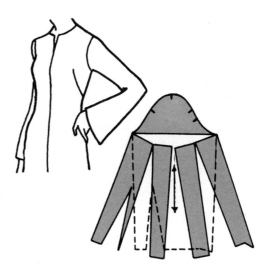

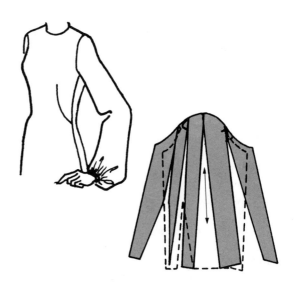

Extend the pattern if a longer or fuller sleeve is required.

Musketeer or mousquetaire sleeve

This is a pretty gathered sleeve where a basic sleeve is cut for the gathered section to be attached. This is usually made of net, chiffon, nylon, silk or any lightweight fabric, as the musketeer type of sleeve is only suitable for soft and pliable materials. If vertical stitching is made to hold the gathers a lining is unnecessary.

Method

Indicate the grain line and slash horizontally.

Divide the sleeve into equal parts.

Cut through the sections and open out the desired amount and pin on to new paper. (Number sections if it will help.)

Chiffons may require more than twice the amount of shirring.

Notches should be indicated both on the lining and the main sleeve so that the gathering is evenly distributed.

Lantern sleeve

This sleeve can be made any length and can be most effective in fine dainty materials with lace insertions or even in stiffer materials such as poult and taffeta. The amount of flare may vary, although the sleeve is usually cut on a circular plan. It should fit without gathering at either the armhole or the cuff.

Method

Trace the block on a new piece of paper.

Mark the length required.

Close the wrist dart.

Decide where the lantern shape is to be and draw a line.

Draw radiating lines from the lantern line to wristline and crown of sleeve.

Slash from the lantern line to within 2 cm of wristline, and spread the sections to create a circle. Overlap at the wrist if necessary.

Slash and open the radiating lines from the lantern line towards crown of sleeve to correspond with lower section.

Lace insertions can be most attractive on this sleeve.

84

Shirtwaister sleeve

Invariably this makes its appearance every season as one of the classic sleeves. It can be cut three-quarter, seven-eighths or full-length and always has a cuff. Any type of cuff can be used, which allows great scope for the creation of something new and original. This style is made up in different weights and thicknesses of material. The width of the sleeve, therefore, will depend upon the fabric used.

Method

Cut as for the bishop sleeve, but first decide the width of cuff and cut off the required amount.

Indicate where the normal dart would be and mark the opening 75 mm (full scale).

Add extra sleeve length if the fullness is required to shape over the cuff. If you want a narrow cuff, this can be cut on the straight and on a fold at the wrist. A wider cuff needs to be shaped as diagram.

Allow the buttonstand on the cuff according to the size of the button. (See p. 145.)

Make the placket or opening in line with the little finger by dividing the lower edge into three, with two-thirds of the width at the front and one third at the back. The cuff of the sleeve is interlined, and requires an underlap and overlap.

Leg o' mutton sleeve

This is a style used in stage production and modified in many ways for ordinary use. The crown can be stiffened to stand away above the shoulder. If greater fullness is required, the crown is heightened and widened. The sleeve can be cut on the bias to give a good tight fit over the forearm, or on the straight. The opening can be decorative, with buttons, as required, while the underarm sleeve length should always be the same length as the original block pattern.

Method

Trace the basic sleeve block on a new piece of paper.

Pin the elbow dart so that you produce a bulge.

Slash from the crown to the elbow as shown.

Spread the slashed sections to give the amount of fullness needed.

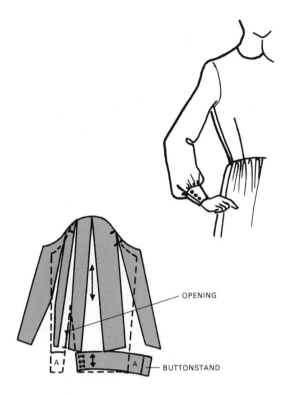

OPENING

BUTTONSTAND

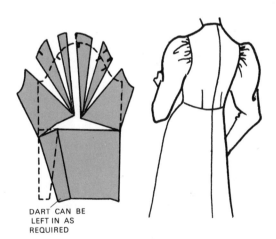

DART CAN BE LEFT IN AS REQUIRED

Make a new pattern by tracing the outline through on another piece of paper, putting in the notches so that the gathers or pleats are put in a position where they can be evenly spaced over the top of the sleeve. Mark the grain, which is usually on the bias or on the straight if the material is soft and pliable.

Kimono sleeve

The kimono sleeve has an Eastern origin. It gives a loose draped appearance around the armhole area and is cut in one with the bodice. A true kimono is cut without a shoulder seam but nowadays it is usually cut with a seam over the shoulder and down the centre of the arm. Soft material which drapes easily is most suitable for this type of sleeve.

Method

Draw a vertical line the length of the sleeve and shoulder.

Move the position of the back shoulder dart to neckline.

Move the position of the front shoulder dart to waistline.

Match and lay side neck points of front and back bodice to top of line leaving a space of 2 cm (full scale) between shoulder points.

Back underarm and front underarm should be level. To check this, square a line from the centre line to these two points.

Arrange the sleeve against the bodice so that the centre line of the sleeve at back and front is in line with the side neck point and the vertical distance between the sleeve and bodice underarms is approximately 3·5 cm (This amount can vary according to the desired angle of the overarm seam.)

Remember that the straighter the overarm seam, the more drape will accumulate under the arm, while a greater slope may have a tendency to restrict the movement of the arm unless a very soft and pliable fabric is used.

From the side seam at the waist to the wristline follow the lines of the diagram and draw a smooth curve.

Check the underarm and overarm seam lengths and then finalise the position of the darts. Trace the back and front separately, taking the length of the sleeve from the side neck point to the wrist line. Lay on new paper and add the necessary seam allowances.

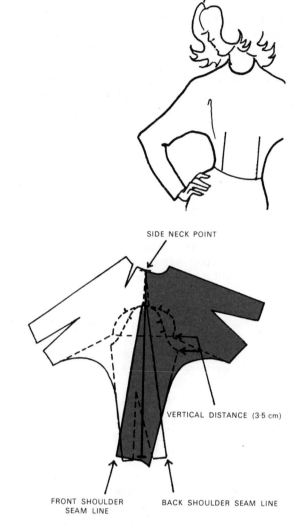

SIDE NECK POINT

VERTICAL DISTANCE (3·5 cm)

FRONT SHOULDER
SEAM LINE

BACK SHOULDER SEAM LINE

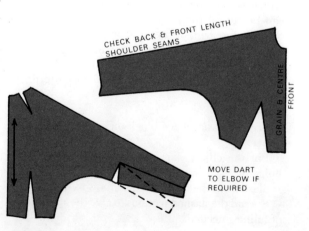

CHECK BACK & FRONT LENGTH
SHOULDER SEAMS

GRAIN & CENTRE FRONT

MOVE DART
TO ELBOW IF
REQUIRED

Dolman sleeve

Dolman sleeves are distinguished from kimono sleeves by the unusually deep and wide armhole seam. The sleeve is in one piece and extends up over the shoulder point position towards the centre of the shoulder. The armhole seam can be cut either square or curved, according to the style. The dolman style is usually drafted from the kimono block and the procedure is the same except for the armhole. Sometimes this sleeve is referred to as the *batwing*. It has a low deep armhole to allow for easy movement. It is used in coats and suits where a roomier and fuller fit is required.

Method

Trace back and front kimono block and lay together along centre line of sleeve.

Mark design line of armhole seam.

Indicate where slashes are required for extra fullness underneath the arm.

Join the front and back sleeve together and cut along armhole seam line.

Slash and spread the desired amount under the arms, and lay on new paper.

Mark round new sleeve shape.

Add all seam allowances and apply balance notches to sleeve and bodice sections.

Close the darts to move them into seam lines if the design stipulates this.

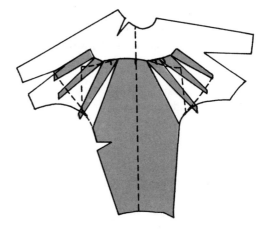

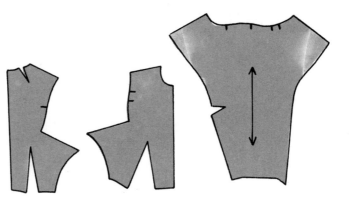

Raglan sleeve

The raglan type sleeve is distinguished by seams running from points from the front and back bodice neckline and joining low down in the armhole. The sleeve can be cut in one section with a dart centre shoulder, or in two sections with a seam running the length of the arm and shoulder. Always check the length of the bodice and sleeve seams. At C the distance between the front sleeve and bodice can vary, depending upon whether a close fit or a draped effect is required.

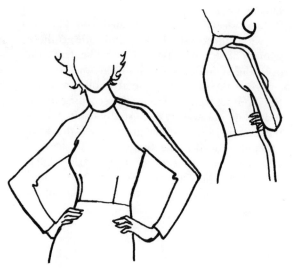

Method

Draw a straight line and lay the centre of the sleeve to this line.

Trace around sleeve.

Lay back bodice to back of sleeve matching the notches. Pivot bodice until the shoulder point overlaps the head of sleeve approximately 1·5 cm (full scale) or 3 mm (one-fifth scale).

Trace around back bodice.

Move front shoulder dart to waist.

Lay front bodice armhole and sleeve pitches level with each other. Pivot bodice until front shoulder point laps sleeve as back.

Trace around front bodice.

Draw raglan line on front and back bodice and mark notches for sleeve and bodice.

Re-shape shoulder seam into dart and notch front and back to allow for easing.

If seam is required down centre of sleeve, allow for seams when cutting.

The back shoulder dart can be moved into the back seam A–B if desired. Make the length from C–D the same for both bodice and sleeve. If there is a variation, compromise – adding a little on, taking a little off until the measurements are identical.

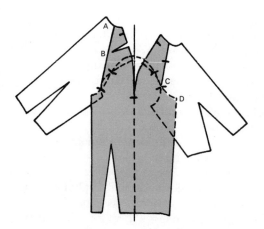

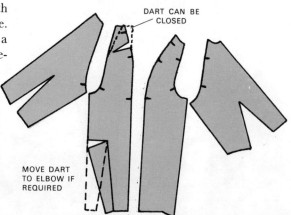

DART CAN BE CLOSED

MOVE DART TO ELBOW IF REQUIRED

Magyar sleeve

Having a gusset these sleeves allow the arms to be raised more easily than do kimono sleeves. When the arm is in its dropped and normal position, the gusset is inconspicuous.

Many shapes of gusset are used with the magyar sleeve and sometimes a garment may be cut with a set-in sleeve effect at the front and a magyar effect at the back, or vice versa.

Experiment with gussets of various kinds and try out new ideas.

By using imagination you can achieve different effects.

Method

Down the centre of the paper draw a line the sleeve and shoulder length.

Lay the centre grain line of the sleeve block to this line and trace the shape of the sleeve.

Measure 6·5 cm (full scale) or 1·3 cm (one-fifth scale) down from the underarm of both sleeve and bodice at back and front. Mark as A and B.

Place the back bodice to the back sleeve and overlap at C.

Match the sleeve and bodice notches as on the raglan sleeve.

Trace around the back bodice block.

Repeat the same process for the front bodice as in the raglan sleeve.

From Point C draw and position a line 11 cm (full scale) or 2·2 cm (one-fifth scale) upwards and towards the intersection of the back bodice and sleeve seam. Mark as D. This is the cut line for the gusset.

Draw line CD on front and back.

On either side of Point C measure down the sleeve and bodice at back and front 2 cm (full scale) or 4 mm (one-fifth scale) to Points E and F.

Join Points D and E and D and F. These are the sewing lines of the gusset.

Lay your set square on line F to D and square a line making G to D the same length as D to F.

Join Points F and G for gusset.

From shoulder points draw a smooth line to centre of sleeve and mark balance points.

Cut through sleeve and add seam allowances.

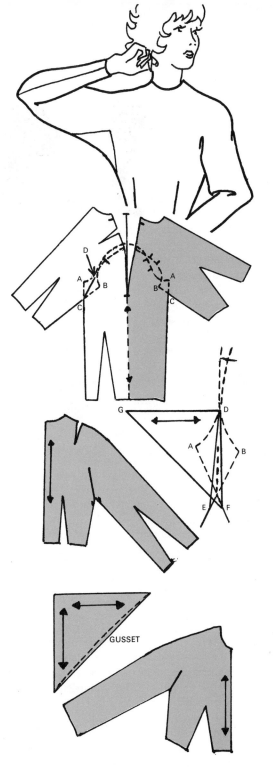

Add the necessary seam allowances for the gusset, and mark the grain line G–D.

To reduce bulk under the arm, curve gusset slightly at maximum length. (See diagram.)

Cuffs should be marked on the block and cut to the shape of the wrist line, especially if a wide cuff is required. Buttoned cuffs require an overlap and an underlap and should follow the natural grain of the sleeve. Notches should be given to match the arm section. Cuffs are usually cut double and should 'clean up' the inside seam of the upper part of the sleeve.

Narrow cuffs are usually cut straight and on the fold at the wristline. The illustrations given are a few which add interest and fashion value to a sleeve.

Collars and Necklines

FLAT

There are three kinds of collar: flat, roll or standing. They can be attached to the neckline, detached or convertible. 'Convertible' means that they can be worn open or closed. The style line – or outer edge line – can be described as Peter Pan, shirt, sailor, shawl, etc. and it is advisable to state whether the collar is flat, medium or high roll. Until you acquire the skill to cut collar patterns, always test your patterns first with cheap material before cutting into expensive cloth.

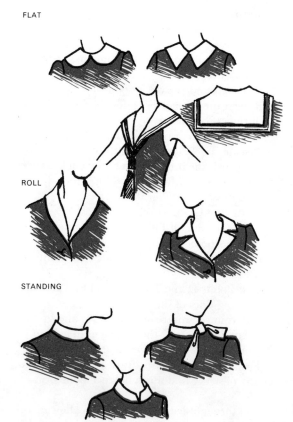

ROLL

If an overlap is required at the front bodice section, this must be done before developing the pattern. Flat collars can be any width from 5 cm to the complete shoulder width, and can be cut to any shaped neckline. Stand collars can be cut and shaped or made from a strip of material cut on the bias and folded over. Roll collars must have a stand and a fall.

STANDING

If a collar is too narrow, the part which rolls over and covers the stand will not be sufficient to conceal it; if it is too wide it will automatically ride up into its natural position and will then give a higher stand than was originally intended.

Parts of a collar

The *breakline* is the line that separates the stand and turnover portions and runs from the collar to the top button of the opening.

The *stand* of a collar is the part that fits close to the back of the neck and is covered by the turnover or fall of collar. It can vary in height above the basic neckline from 1 cm to 5 cm and more, depending upon the requirements of the design.

The *fall* or *turnover* is the part which falls over the stand and becomes part of the outer surface of the garment.

The *style line* is the outer edge of the collar and can be cut to any shape as required.

The neck edge of the collar influences the roll. If the neck edge is similar in shape to the neckline of the garment, the collar will be almost flat. If less curved, or even straight at the neck edge, the collar will roll and create its stand.

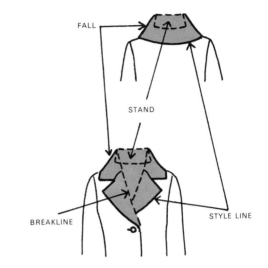

Points to remember when designing collars

1 A neckline must be perfectly shaped before you design the collar. It should not be stretched or tight and should lie flat on the body without any wrinkles.

2 Make sure the basic design of the collar is good before adding any decorative details.

3 It is safer to determine the silhouette of a collar on a dress stand than on a flat table. After the correct line and proportions have been established, then the pattern can be corrected and finally cut.

4 Under-collars are always drafted first and the top collars are usually made larger, according to the material used.

5 It is usual to notch the centre back and the neck points of a collar.

6 The average amount used for a collar stand is 2·5 cm. A higher and closer necked collar requires 4 cm. This will vary according to design requirements.

Various collars

Peter Pan collar (flat)
Method
1 Close the shoulder darts, using the back and front bodice block. Overlap at shoulder points 1·5 cm. Match the neck points.
2 Re-define neckline at centre front and drop 3 cm.
3 Check neck circle of garment and collar. Reduce collar slightly at centre front as necessary. The curve of the collar neckline should differ from the neck circle to create a very small roll to hide the seam line.

Tailored collar (roll)
Method
First decide size of button, mark centre front line and buttonstand. Measure half back neck of pattern.
1 Extend shoulder line 5 mm to 0. Draw a line through this point level with the top buttonhole, extending it from O to A, the measurement of half back neck of pattern.
   This line is called the breakline and the lapel and part of the collar roll on this line.
2 To lower the roll, pivot AX line required amount. (See dotted AX line.)
3 Check the back neck measurement again to A from O line.
4 Square a line from second breakline for the centre back of the collar, so that AB equals the stand of the collar (5 mm one-fifth scale and 2·5 cm full scale) and AC equals the fall of the collar (1·5 cm one-fifth scale and 7·5 cm full scale) (Diagram is squared from dotted AX line.)
5 Join BX in good curve. Draw line for collar outer edge from C to centre front line, to required style line.

The difference between the stand and the fall is usually the position where the second breakline will be. This is essentially a fitted collar and it is suitable for jackets. It is the basis for all well fitting collars.

For dressy collars a strip of the desired length and width can be cut, provided the neckline corresponds with the neckline of the garment. The centre back can be cut on either a convex

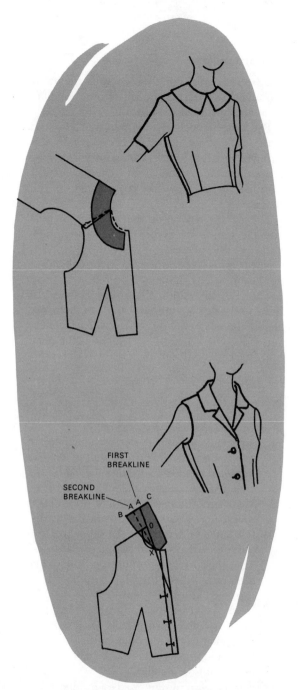

Note: The second breakline is where the collar actually rolls. If it rolled on the first breakline it would be too high.

or concave curve and graduated towards the centre front. This will give quite a neat collar if the average 2·5 cm stand is given for full scale garments.

Shawl collar (roll)

Method

First decide size of button, mark centre front line and buttonstand. Measure half back neck of pattern.

1   Draw a line through the side neck point B level with the top buttonhole, extending it from B to A the measurement of half back neck of pattern. This is the breakline.

2   Join C to B so that BC is same measurement as AB and AC is squared from BC.

3   Square a line from BC line for the centre back of the collar, so that AC equals the stand of the collar (5 mm one-fifth scale and 2·5 cm full scale) and AD equals the fall of the collar (1·1 cm one-fifth scale and 5·5 cm full scale).

4   Draw a line from D to E. This is the style line of the collar and it can be slashed as the second diagram shows if a lower roll is desired.

The centre back collar can be squared at different angles for lower rolled effects, by varying the angle of the breakline at AB as the third diagram shows.

The seam of this collar is centre back but the top collar can be cut on the fold and the facing grown on.

Mandarin collar (stand)

First method

Draw an oblong shape half the neck measurement and 3 cm wide (full scale) or 6 mm (one-fifth scale). Indicate Points A, B and C and the centre back.

Point C is raised 2 cm (full scale) or 4 mm (one-fifth scale) above B.

Draw a smooth curve from A to C for the neckline and make equal widths from the centre back to the centre front. Shape centre front edge to C according to the design.

Second method

Cut a strip half the neck measurement and the width required. Draw and slash the lines as on the diagram. Overlap the slashed sections approximately 1 cm (full scale) or 2 mm (one-fifth scale).

Lay the band on a new piece of paper and re-cut the pattern, adding all the turnings.

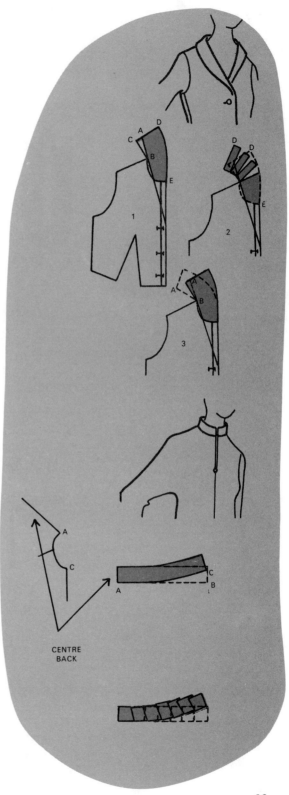

Jabots

The jabot is used as an accessory and is a variation of the circular flounce. It can also be cut in one with the collar.

Materials which drape easily are suitable for this neckline.

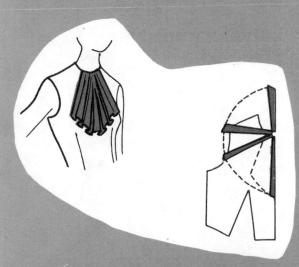

Method
1 Draw the outline of the jabot on the bodice and trace it on to a fresh piece of paper.
2 Slash and spread as required.
3 Draw a smooth outline of the new shape and cut the pattern, adding the necessary turnings. The grain line is usually the same as for the basic bodice.

Questions and Project

1 Using your one-fifth scale blocks illustrate and describe how you would produce (a) a raglan sleeve (b) a magyar sleeve (c) a kimono sleeve.
2 Sketch the following collars and illustrate how you would pattern them: (a) convertible (b) bertha (c) turtle.
3 Show by sketch and diagram how you would construct the pattern for each of the following: (a) a semi-flared eight-gored skirt (b) a button-through skirt, slightly flared with a patch pocket (c) a graduated pleated skirt with pleats commencing at the waistline.
4 Produce in one-fifth scale and then full scale a princess style dress.
5 Discuss the effect of vertical, horizontal and diagonal lines as style features in dress design. Sketch and pattern one day dress illustrating one of the above features.
6 Illustrate and pattern three variations of the sleeves given in this book.
7 Pattern and illustrate a dress with a cowl neckline, the cowl to be inset into the front bodice of the garment. Suggest the material to be used for this style.
8 Sketch a garment with a yoke effect. Explain the basic function of a yoke and illustrate how you would pattern the garment.
9 Why is fullness required in a set-in sleeve head?
   Discuss in detail the effect in wear of a sleeve with no fullness allowed in a normal armhole.
10 Sketch and pattern two day dresses, illustrating the latest fashion line employed by a leading couturier designer, yet suitable for the requirements of the British ready-to-wear market.
11 Write out your own personal size chart giving both body and finished measurements.
12 Make a basic shirtwaister dress to your own design, incorporating the following features: roll collar, buttoned front bodice, full-length sleeves with cuff, yoked back bodice.

Trousers

Trouser-cutting is an art and it is impossible to make a block which will conform to everyone's personal measurements. The stature, thickness and variation at the crutch and the thigh produce many fitting variables. It is only with experience in fitting the individual that you can hope to attain a professional standard.

Cut and make as many garments as possible, allowing ample turnings for alterations.

Parts of the trouser

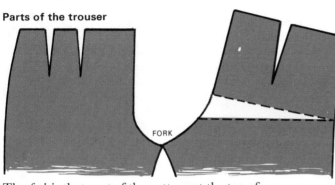

The *fork* is that part of the pattern at the top of the inside leg between the front and back of the seat.

The seam line towards the centre front waist is the *front fork line*.

The crotch or crutch refers to the body and is the part of the figure at the top of the thighs between the front and back of the seat.

The *seat line* is the line from the fork to the top waist line, on the underpart on the centre back.

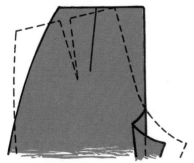

The *seat angle*, the seat line on the pattern, is not cut vertically but at an angle (approximately 15°, but variable). When this line assumes the vertical on the figure it creates a small fold in the material. This fold gives ease when the body bends forward.

Making the block

Trousers

Waist 66 cm   Hips 96   Length 100

Formula: $\frac{1}{6}$ $\frac{1}{4}$ $\frac{1}{3}$ of hip measurement.

(*or* One-fifth scale: Waist 13·2   Hips 19·2   Length 20)

Trouser front

Draw foundation line, 2 cm from right hand side of paper.

		One-fifth scale cm	Full scale cm
0–1	Waist to ankle	20	100
0–2	Waist to hip	4	20
0–3	Waist to crutch	5	25
0–4	Waist to knee (half of 3–1)	7·5	37·5
0–5	$\frac{1}{6}$ of hip measurement	3·2	16
0–6	$\frac{1}{4}$ of hip measurement	4·8	24
3–7	$\frac{1}{3}$ of hip measurement	6·4	32

0–1, 0–2, 0–3, 0–4 Draw in horizontal lines from 0–1 line.

0–5, 0–6 Draw in vertical lines parallel to 0–1.

7–8   Junction of 6 and 3
8–9   Take previous measurement at 90° angle.

From 6 (centre front waist) draw line downwards to 2 line and then curve to 9 and then 7.

This is the front fork.

5–11 and 5–12 Either side of 5 line measure half of ankle width.

0–10 and 10–11 Shape side seams. Draw curve to 2 then straight to width required at ankle.

12A   Approximately halfway between 3 and 4 lines, depending on thickness of thigh. This completes the front trouser.

12A: ·5 (one-fifth scale), 2·5 (full scale)

7–12A–12 Curve to 12A then straight to ankle width.

Trouser back

From 2 measure to junction of 6 and 2

2–13   Swing an arc of that measurement

13–13A   Draw line from 2 at 15° angle, usually the required amount for the seat angle, to intersect arc from 2–13.

For this pattern

13A–14   Lay the set square at an angle of 90° to the intersection and square, raising the centre back waist the same amount as the wedge. Join 0–14.

13A–14: 2·5 (one-fifth scale), 2·5 (full scale)

7–8A   Half measurement of 7–8

7–8A: 1·5 (one-fifth scale), 2·5 (full scale)

7–15   Same distance as 7–8A minus 4 mm (one-fifth scale) 2 cm (full scale)

15–13A–14 Join in a good smooth line.

15–12A Follow line of 7–12A as illustrated then to 12

0–2   Follow line of 10–2 as illustrated then to 11.

Mark position of darts to conform with waistline. The back darts should be parallel to 14 line.

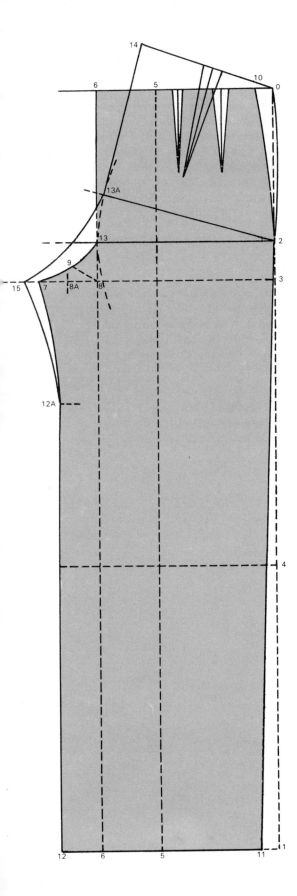

After completing the block in size 12 measurements, try drafting a block to your own personal measurements.

Have all your measurements written down in the following order:

1. Length from waist to ankle
2. Hip depth
3. Crutch depth
4. Knee length approximately halfway between crutch and ankle
5. Hip measurement
6. Waist measurement
7. Width around knee (check measurement, otherwise use method employed in drafting the pattern)
8. Width around ankle
9. Have your basic skirt block available.

Note: People with small seats would not require a 15° angle. The amount will vary according to a person's dimensions and stature.

If a closer fitting style of trouser is desired this is achieved by graduating the inside leg and side seams from the hipline.

Lingerie

The hard wear and frequent laundering of undergarments demand materials which will be durable yet fine and dainty. The styles should be simple, while the seaming should be sufficiently strong to withstand constant washing. Laces and trimmings should be as durable as the main garment. The lingerie block is based on the princess line, but with careful thought many adaptations can be made to create an endless variety of designs.

The material used will influence the tolerance allowed on the pattern, and for woven cloths it is advisable to cut the sections on the bias. Jersey materials (circular knitted) are suitable for cutting on the straight grain, as they will stretch to the body shape.

Making a lingerie block

Method applying to any basic block

Lay bodice and skirt blocks together as for a princess line dress. The centre back of the bodice and skirt should touch. The centre front bodice and skirt should overlap at the basic waist line.

Reduce tolerances to ease body measurements, allowing the garment to slip over the body easily and yet fit well over the bustline.

Begin by drawing a line for the bra section opening the dart two and a half times the normal amount. O is positioned above the bust line.

Note: Different seam allowances are made for woven fabrics compared with those for jersey knits. Woven fabrics are cut on the bias, while jersey cloths are cut on the straight grain, provided they are circular knit.

		One-fifth scale cm	Full scale cm
0–1	This line can vary.	1·2	6
0–2	Draw line to dart.	2·4	12
2A–3	Curve to underarm and drop, 2 and 2A should be level.	·5	2·5
3–4	Reduce width and define horizontal seam line.		
Join 4–5–5A and then 1, 5 and 5A should be level. Join 2–5A and 2A–5			
1–6	Below bust line to centre front waist.		
7–8	Half of front bust dart.		
8–9	Half of 7–8.		
9–10	Draw line parallel to centre front.		
5A–7–11	Front seam line. Flare as required.		
5–8–12	Front seam line. Flare as required.		
4–13–14	Flare side seam as for gored skirt.		
3A–15–16	Flare side seam as for gored skirt, 3 and 3A should be level		
3A to 17	Raise centre back above bust line	·3	1·5
19–20	Extend the centre back. (This can vary) and raise.	·8	4
		·3	1·5
Join 17–18–19 for completion of back skirt.			

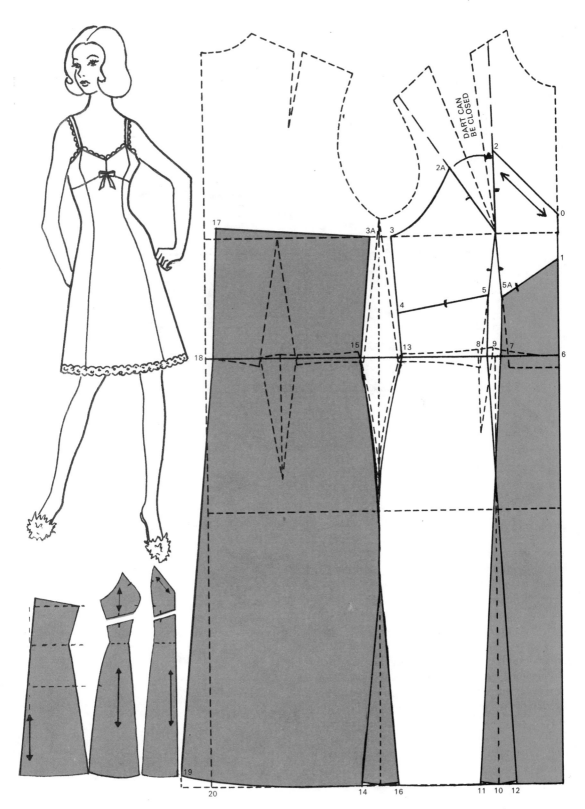

DART CAN
BE CLOSED

2
2A
0
1
17
3A 3
5 5A
4
15 13 8 9 7
18 6
19
20 14 16 11 10 12

99

Brief and hipster block from basic skirt block

Method

Lay back and front side seams together, over-lapping if necessary to reduce tolerance.

Trace waistline, eliminating darts.

Define crutchline 5·2 cm (one-fifth scale) or 26 cm (full scale) below centre front waist and drop 1·3 cm (one-fifth scale) or 6·5 cm (full scale) and mark point A.

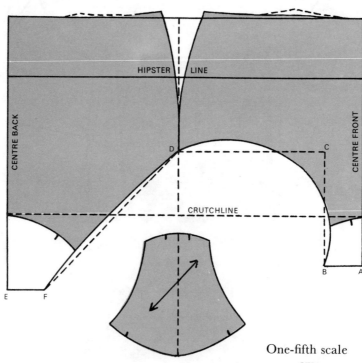

		One-fifth scale cm	Full scale cm
A–B	Square line for fork.	1	5
B–C	Square upwards to C.	3	15
	Complete to D at side seam.		
E	Below crutchline at centre back.	2	10
E–F	Square for fork.	1	5
F–D	Join for back leg opening.		

Draw smooth curve, as shown in the diagram, joining both back and front fork sections. If a gusset is required, indicate on the pattern the position of the gusset. Trace sections and re-cut. Gussets are usually cut on the bias and on the double. For hipster briefs reduce the length from waistline 1·6 cm (one-fifth scale) or 8 cm (full scale).

Shorts can be cut on the trouser principle.

Pattern Alterations

Altering bought patterns

Never slash into a pattern hastily. Visualise what effect a particular position will have in relation to the result you want, then cut after you have measured. You can then adjust as you think fit. With practice in making and fitting patterns you will become quick at noting where a ready-made pattern is at fault for a particular wearer. Slight alterations can be made without throwing the whole of the pattern out of proportion, but changes should be made where they least alter the outline of the pattern. Patterns are usually enlarged or shortened in the same area.

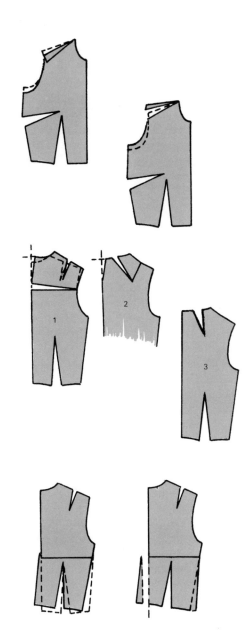

Alteration for sloping shoulders
Slash the back and front approximately 3 cm down on the armhole edge, almost to the neckline. Lap the edges of the slash, tapering to nothing at the neck edge. Lower the armhole slightly to correspond with the sleeve head.

Alteration for square shoulders
Slash the front and back 3 cm approximately down from the shoulder point and cut to neckline. Spread the required amount and add an equal amount to the underarm curve, keeping the same armhole shaping.

Alteration for round shoulders
1 Slash the pattern across the back, halfway between the neck and depth of arm scye. Spread the required amount. Re-define the centre back line.
2 Move shoulder dart to neck.
3 Put the excess neck width into the neck dart, positioning the apex of the dart where necessary. Match the back and front shoulders.

Alteration for short back balance
Very often an over-erect figure has a posture which results in a hollow back. Horizontal wrinkles occur across the back towards the underarm. You can remedy this by folding the surplus amount from the centre back towards the underarm. Re-define the centre back line and add the amount taken off at the centre back to the underarm line if needed.

Large bust

A large high bust is frequently due to over-erect posture. Diagonal wrinkles appear from the bust line to the underarm seam. Remedy this by slashing the pattern from the centre front along the bust line to the underarm edge and then cut upwards towards the shoulder edge and downwards towards the waistline edge, opening the slashes the necessary amount. Re-draw the centre front line and if necessary add extra to the waistline if the side seam darts need to be deepened. Either one or two darts can be used, but the apex of the dart should come in line with the point of the bust.

Small bust

If a figure is very slight, with an unusually small bust, wrinkles may form horizontally across the bust line.

Put this right by making the darts shallower and lift the front at the shoulder, re-defining the front neckline, shoulder and armhole curve. Adjust the sleeve.

Large upper arm

Careful observation will help you decide whether to alter for the full length or for the upper arm only. If for the full length, slash on centre line from the top to the bottom of the full length of sleeve and open the amount needed. If for the upper part only, slash on centre line to the elbow and either side along elbow line to underarm edges. Open to the extent you need. For very large arms extra material may have to be added to the underarm seam. The size of the armhole must be changed to accommodate the enlarged sleeve. Usually the pattern is slashed across the chest and centre back and opened out. The depth of scye can be deepened, but only slightly; otherwise there will be a strain on the sleeve.

Sleeve incorrectly balanced

Owing to the posture of the figure a sleeve often needs to be 'repitched'. Diagonal wrinkles occur and the sleeve must have the balance marks moved until the twist in the sleeve is corrected. Alter notches on the sleeve and lift either one or two centimetres.

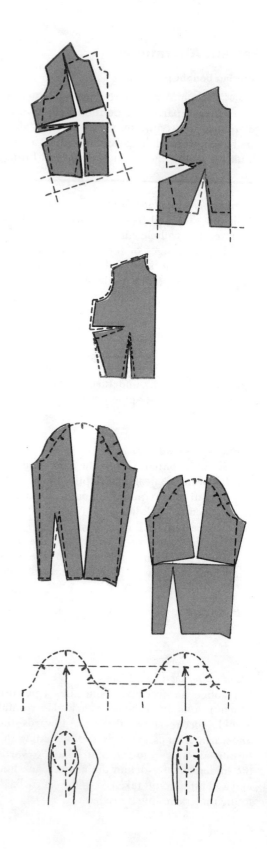

Large abdomen

Slash the skirt front vertically to approximately 15 cm below the waistline. Slash horizontally to the side edge and vertically to the hem line. Cut from centre front horizontally to slash. Spread the slashed parts the amount you need, tapering from centre front to side seam and from waistline towards hemline. Surplus at waist can be added to original dart or divided into two darts as best suited to figure. If required in the bodice too, then slash vertically from waist to shoulder and centre front to side seam.

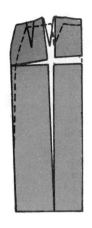

Hollow back

Fold the pattern below the back waist as much as necessary. Re-define the centre back line and dart. Make a smooth curve at the back waist.

Prominent hip

Add the amount needed at the hipline and take in the surplus at the waistline by deepening the dart or making two darts. Add extra width at waistline by adding to the side seam. Add extra length if necessary.

Balance of the skirt

When the side seam slants towards the back the cause may be the posture of the person or over-developed hip muscles. Wrinkles may occur diagonally from the centre front to the side seam. Alter by lifting the front and straightening the side seam. Re-define the centre front line and re-curve the waistline.

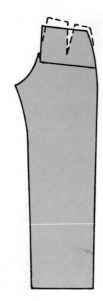

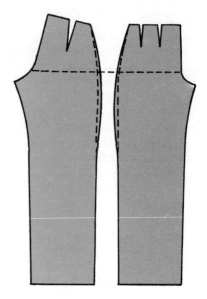

Slacks:
Too long in the back seat
Reduce from the centre back to the side seam by folding a tuck to take up the surplus material. Re-define dart.

Thick thighs
These give rise to wrinkles across the front crutch. Add an extra amount to the hipline of both front and back sections.

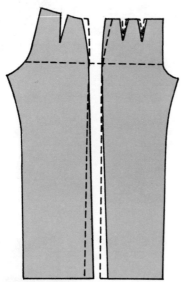

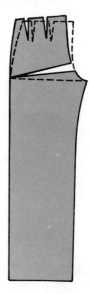

Side seam balance
If the seam is slanting towards the back, allow extra on the front side seam from the waist to the hip and deepen the front dart. When added to the side seam at the front it must be deducted from the back. From the hip to the ankle, deduct surplus from the front section and add to the back.

Fork too tight
This trouble is caused by the thickness of the body, or a large abdomen and makes diagonal wrinkles from the crutch towards the front waistline. Insufficient allowance has been made for the fork part of the trouser. Re-define the crutch part of the trouser, as shown on the diagram.

PART 4 CUTTING AND MAKING GARMENTS

Choosing the Fabrics
Suitable fabric for the style and the occasion

Nowadays the range of fabrics from which to choose a suitable cloth for a particular style is so wide that it is bewildering. Sometimes it can result in a waste of money if you choose unwisely. The knowledge you have gained from collecting scraps of material and trying to identify them should enable you to choose the right fabric for any style. To test your skill and design sense, a collection of garments has been sketched so that you can experiment and see which material you would select for the various designs. These are not high fashion designs, but the basic 'bread and butter numbers' found in many shops. Remember that the garment design determines which *textures* will be used, while the finish will make a great difference in *fabric performance*. It is sensible, therefore, to handle the material lightly to test its properties. In other words, get the feel of the cloth, especially if you want it to drape.

Before making the final selection ask yourself the following questions:

1 On what occasion would the garment be worn?
2 Does the cloth complement the style?
3 Is the material washable?
4 Is the material crease-resistant?
5 Is the material flame-resistant?
   (This applies especially to children's wear.)
6 Has it been pre-shrunk?
7 Is it off-grain?
8 Is it worth the money?
9 Will it wear well?
10 Is it suitable for the wearer's skin?

Design project

When your selection is complete, sketch each style again, making your own interpretation. For instance, you may want bead-work instead of embroidery for the dinner dress or you may wish to use different textures, such as corduroy, for the trouser suit and crêpe for the blouse. For the shirtwaister dress you may prefer to use stitching or tucking to decorate. Apply your own individual touch and put a swatch of the material you have chosen on each of the sketches. If you decide to cut the patterns yourself leave a space for remarks about any difficulties you experience. Write down any special details of the interfacings and linings used – the size of buttons, the type of embroidery, the width of lace, the width of petersham (if any), the quantity of material, its cost per metre and any other expenses incurred. Then study the following details of making.

Interfacings

To achieve a professional appearance most garments require an interfacing. This is an extra piece of specially-made material placed between the outer fabric of the garment and the facing. It adds body to the garment, where crispness, stiffness or firmness is required and often more than one kind of interfacing is used in a garment. It is essential where buttons and buttonholes are used.

Depending upon the main material, the interfacings can be washable and dry cleanable but must certainly be pre-shrunk before use. They should never be heavier than the garment material. Woven interfacings are usually cut on the same grain as the outer fabric, but there are occasions when the grain line is altered to prevent stretching. Non-woven interfacings can be cut in any direction, as they have no grain and they do not fray. Fusible interfacings or iron-on interfacings can be woven or non-woven and should be used only on fabrics which are firm enough, so that the outline is not visible on the right side of the garment. Conventional interfacings are usually attached by tacking or basting, or are machined in with the facings. Fusible interfacings are generally produced from thin material over which a fusible adhesive is distributed, either in dots or in a random pattern. In the operation of fusing the interfacing to the main garment, heat is applied to soften the adhesive, in order to allow bonding to take place.

The grain on linings and interfacings
Every section of pattern should have the *grain line* marked. In many garments the grain line of the interfacing is altered to counteract the stretching of the cloth. If a neckline is cut on the bias grain, the interfacing is cut on the straight grain to prevent stretching at the neck edge. This applies to many garments made on the bias; if a lining is used it is very often cut on the straight grain of the fabric. This holds and keeps the particular sections in their correct shape and so prevents any distortion. Interfacings can also be cut to the fold-line of the garment, machine or herring-bone stitched to the main material depending upon the fabric. For thick, open weave material the latter would be suitable.

Interfacing for garments with bound or piped buttonholes
Place interfacing to the wrong side of the garment. Work the buttonholes through the interfacing.

Interfacing for all other garments
Generally, place the interfacing so that seam turnings are behind the interfacing when the garment is worn, to prevent the seam impression from showing on the right side. According to the design and fabric choice therefore, the interfacing can be placed to the wrong side of the garment or facing.

Interfacing machine-stitched in place
Stitch along seam line on edges to be seamed. Stitch along fold line of grown-on facing, but end stitching at breakline for garments with turn-back collar, rever etc., so that the stitching will not show on the right side of the garment (see diag: (a)).

Stitch close to outer edges of facing if required (see diagram (a))
or :
Stitch 1 cm from outer edges of facing; trim interfacing close to stitching. Turn outer edges of facing over interfacing and stitch (see diagram (b)).

Interfacing herringbone stitched in place
Generally only suitable for thick or heavy-weight open weave fabrics, it is used on any edge of interfacing which is to a fold in the finished garment (see diagram (c)).

Important for all interfacing
1 Trim away all outer corners of interfacing after seaming through interfacing.
2 Trim away interfacing at hem edges to reduce bulk.
3 Trim away interfacing at zipper opening edges beyond seam lines to reduce bulk.
4 After stitching seams through interfacing, trim interfacing close to stitching to reduce bulk.

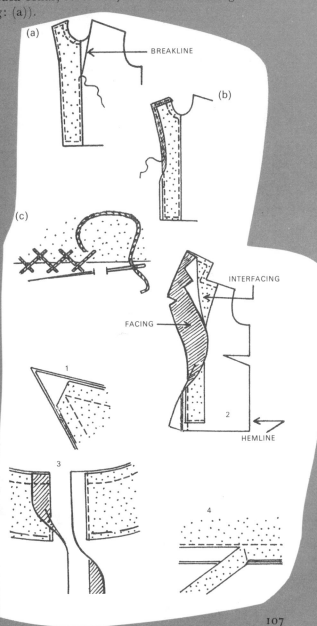

1   What should you consider when making your choice of interfacing?
2   State the interfacings you would use on the garments shown on p. 105.
3   Do they all require interfacings? If so, why?
4   Where would you apply the shape stabilisation?
5   What is the advantage of a woven interfacing over a non-woven?
6   On what grain would you cut the interfacing?
7   Would you apply adhesive interfacings to silk jerseys? If not, why?
8   Where would you use stay tapes?
9   What would you use to strengthen gussets, shaped corners, curved cuffs?
10 Make a list of twelve different interfacings and their particular characteristics.

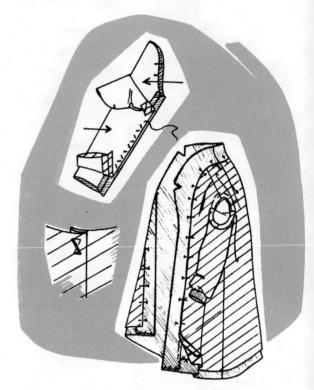

Linings

Linings help to maintain shape, preserve the foundation and take a share of the strain of the garment. They also help in the putting on and taking off of garments, as the lining normally has a glossy finish and so does not 'stick'. In wear, the main material usually stretches, but a lining does not; that is why extra length is required, while width must be given to allow for vigorous movement that might tear the lining. Garments can be lined, half-lined or partly lined. The purpose is:

1   To prevent stretching.
2   To lengthen wear.
3   To prevent irritation to the skin.
4   To neaten the inside.

Linings for coats and suits
Linings need to be cut generously for coats and suits. A tight lining will cause discomfort and distortion to the original garment and the lining is liable to split, especially if a firm taffeta is used. The lower edge of the lining when turned under should overlap the hem of the jacket or coat. Sleeve linings should have extra length; they should be easy, with no restrictions. The lining should be caught to the seams of the sleeves with loose catch-stitches.

Sleeves can be lined first before being attached to the main garment. In more expensive garments a pleat is usually made in the centre back neck, tapering to nothing at the hemline. A soft pleat or easing is given at the centre front shoulder, while waist darts are usually machined but do not fit the garment tightly.

Skirts can have full or half-linings and sometimes a section is put in the back only, to prevent seating. However, this method is not advisable for an expensive garment.

Dresses and jackets

Linings cut as the main material, stitched up as a separate garment and then finally attached to the main body by machining right sides together, are called 'bagged out' garments. In the edge-stitching process a small gap of approximately 16 to 20 cm is left open in either the sleeve or the centre hemline. The garment is drawn through the gap and afterwards the gap is slip-stitched together. Where cowls and drapes are concerned, linings are often cut as the basic block.

Questions

1 Give three examples of materials liable to irritate the skin.
2 Give three examples of materials where lining would be invaluable.
3 What lining material would you use for the garments in the project?
4 Some garments require a 'backing'. In your opinion which garments may need this?

Trimmings

Functional trimmings

Knowing the basic properties of the fabrics used in the garments will allow you to make a correct selection of suitable sewing threads, press studs, belting, boning, elastic, hooks and eyes, zips, buckles and buttons. These are functional trimmings that go into the garment for fastening and finish.

Snap fastenings are used where there is no strain.

Weights are used to assist the hang of the garment.

Questions

1 Name three kinds of weights and state where you would attach them.
2 Make a list of all the types of zips you see advertised and state their purpose.
3 Can you think of any garments not requiring fasteners or openings?
4 How would you reinforce a button?
5 When would you use boning?
6 Where would you use hooks and eyes?

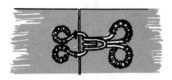

Decorative and ornamental trimmings

In some seasons decoration is out of favour; in other seasons the use of trimmings and decoration is much in vogue. Decoration and ornament therefore depend largely upon the prevailing fashion.

Decoration includes beading, tucking, pleating, embroidery, appliqué, braiding, stitching and also the use of printed fabrics. These are applied to give balance and attractiveness to the garment and add to its beauty and distinction.

Ornaments include jewellery, buckles, buttons, flowers, belts, tassels and rouleaux. They are applied to give emphasis to a particular line, or individuality to the garment, to be eye-catching and yet they must be in good taste.

Trimmings must harmonise with the materials on which they will be used, or act as a contrast to the cloth. Study carefully the question of trimmings and before using them, ask yourself the following questions:

1 Is trimming really necessary for the desired effect?
2 Would it help to accentuate the line, the colour and the fabric?
3 Is the trimming appropriate to the main material?
4 Is it an improvement to the whole garment?

Carefully chosen and wisely-applied trimmings can add to the value of the garment and many attractive results can be obtained.

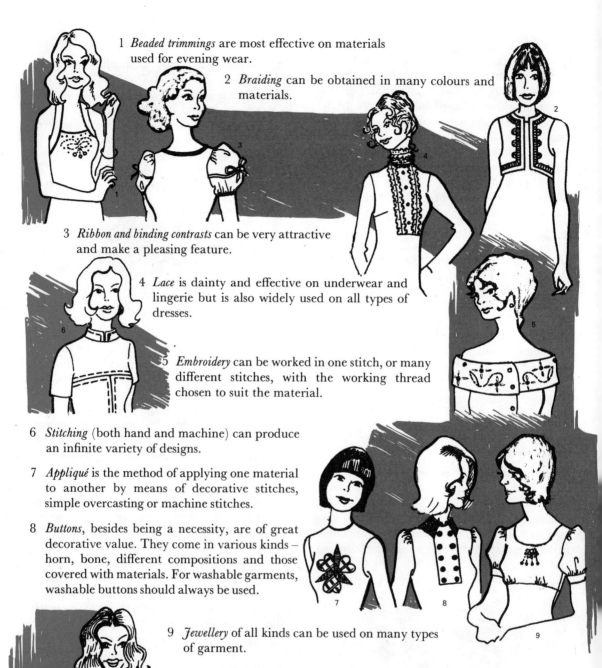

1 *Beaded trimmings* are most effective on materials used for evening wear.

2 *Braiding* can be obtained in many colours and materials.

3 *Ribbon and binding contrasts* can be very attractive and make a pleasing feature.

4 *Lace* is dainty and effective on underwear and lingerie but is also widely used on all types of dresses.

5 *Embroidery* can be worked in one stitch, or many different stitches, with the working thread chosen to suit the material.

6 *Stitching* (both hand and machine) can produce an infinite variety of designs.

7 *Appliqué* is the method of applying one material to another by means of decorative stitches, simple overcasting or machine stitches.

8 *Buttons*, besides being a necessity, are of great decorative value. They come in various kinds – horn, bone, different compositions and those covered with materials. For washable garments, washable buttons should always be used.

9 *Jewellery* of all kinds can be used on many types of garment.

10 *Buckles* can be both functional and decorative.

When applying any ornament, stand in front of the full-length mirror in the garment, to obtain a true perspective and to achieve the desired effect.

11 *Flowers* (*not illustrated*) may be made in a wide variety of materials.

Ribbon trimmings

Ribbons have three uses – to finish, to decorate and to supply colour. They may contrast in colour with the garment, or they may match the material.

SHELL EDGING
(Allow one and a half times required length)

Ribbon can be applied flat, ruffled or pleated. Bows and rosettes of ribbon are used most seasons on all types of garment. When selecting ribbon remember that soft, light-weight ribbons are best for short loops. Grosgrain or stiff ribbons are best for flat bows, while stiff satin or taffeta is best for large tied bows. When measuring ribbon for ruffled trimmings allow one and a half times the length of the finished trimming.

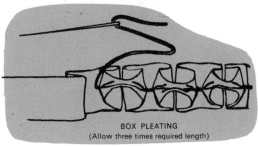

BOX PLEATING
(Allow three times required length)

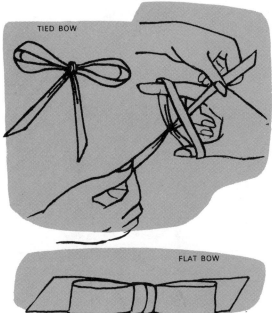

TIED BOW

Different kinds of ribbons
Sarcenet – taffeta weave; *oriental* – taffeta with a satin edge; *satin boyeau* – single satin with a cotton edge; *galloons* – ribbed with continuous edges; *taille* – fine ribbed appearance with bright selvedges; *ciré* – produced by wax and heat and two rollers travelling at different speeds (basically satin); *petersham* – heavily ribbed ribbon; *double satin* – satin both sides.

FLAT BOW

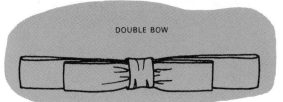

DOUBLE BOW

III

Fringes, tassels and braids

These were first used as trimmings on ancient Egyptian costumes and today we still see fringes, tassels and braids according to the whims of fashion.

Pompoms are used on the ends of cords for tying garments at either neckline or waistline. Cut two discs of cardboard and place together, punch or cut a hole in the middle and wind wool through and round until the cardboard is covered. Snip through the outer edges and then tie cord or several strands in between the loosened discs, pull tightly together and then fluff up the edges to make a ball.

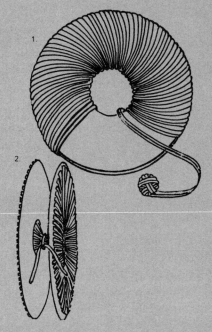

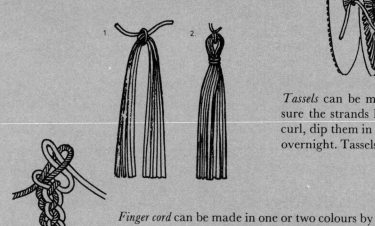

Tassels can be made in a similar way, but be sure the strands hang straight. If they tend to curl, dip them in water and leave them to hang overnight. Tassels need to be attached to a cord.

Finger cord can be made in one or two colours by knitting two threads or groups of threads together and working upwards. First make a loop as illustrated with one colour and then a loop with the other, inserting the one loop into the other and pulling them tight.

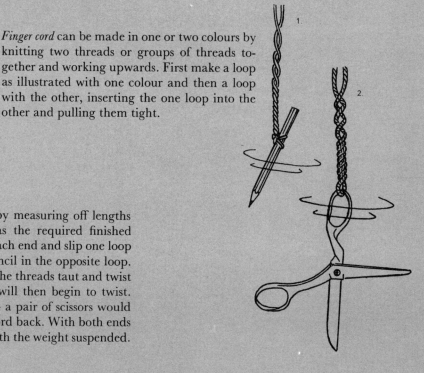

Twisted cord is made by measuring off lengths three times as long as the required finished cord. Knot a loop at each end and slip one loop over a hook, and a pencil in the opposite loop. Stand away and hold the threads taut and twist the pencil. The cord will then begin to twist. Hang a weight on it – a pair of scissors would do – and double the cord back. With both ends over the hook, twist with the weight suspended.

Decorative stitches

Drawn thread work consists of pulling out parallel threads of fabric to obtain an open space, and then hemstitching the edges of this space down to hold the remaining threads securely. It may be used for trimming on any part of a garment. Medium weight linen, heavy linen or sheer materials are suitable for this work. The thread must always be suitable for the fabric.

Hemstitching secures the hem, strengthens the edges and ties the loose threads into bunches. At the open space at each corner a buttonhole stitch is worked close together until the loose threads are reached again. Work from right to left, pass the needle under four open threads, then back behind the same thread and space again, then draw up the threads and repeat the process.

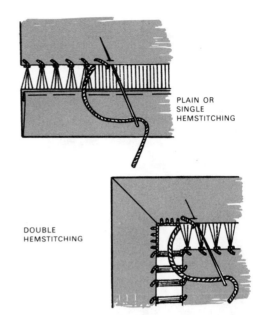

PLAIN OR SINGLE HEMSTITCHING

DOUBLE HEMSTITCHING

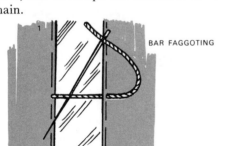

Lazy daisy stitch consists of bringing the needle through the centre, holding the thread down, putting the needle back into the same hole, and bringing it out at the top.

Chain stitch uses the same method as lazy daisy stitch, but the loops are continued to form a chain.

BAR FAGGOTING

Faggoting is a method of joining together any open seams. Regularity of spacing and the same tension throughout are essential. Turn the raw edges of material under and tack both edges to a strip of stout brown paper, leaving a space between. This can vary in width from 6 mm to 1·5 cm, according to preference.

TWISTED FAGGOTING

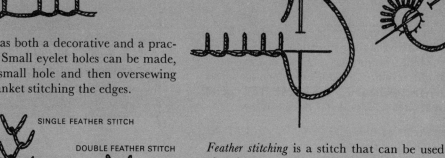

Blanket stitch has both a decorative and a practical purpose. Small eyelet holes can be made, by cutting a small hole and then oversewing first before blanket stitching the edges.

SINGLE FEATHER STITCH

DOUBLE FEATHER STITCH

Feather stitching is a stitch that can be used on closed seams for decorative and practical purposes.

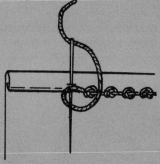

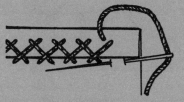

Coral stitch is another stitch for decorating hems and at the same time firmly securing them.

Herring-bone stitch is used for both thick and fine materials.

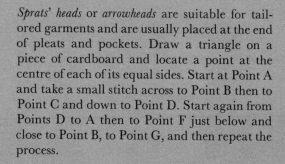

Decorative stitches can be made on the modern machines of today and most attractive results obtained in the finishing of seams and hems and as decoration.

Sprats' heads or *arrowheads* are suitable for tailored garments and are usually placed at the end of pleats and pockets. Draw a triangle on a piece of cardboard and locate a point at the centre of each of its equal sides. Start at Point A and take a small stitch across to Point B then to Point C and down to Point D. Start again from Points D to A then to Point F just below and close to Point B, to Point G, and then repeat the process.

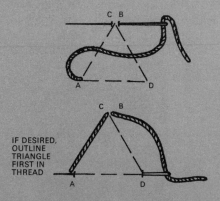

IF DESIRED, OUTLINE TRIANGLE FIRST IN THREAD

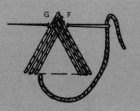

Smocking and shirring

Smocking has been used throughout the centuries as a decorative method of gathering together a wide piece of material in regular folds. Today with modern machines it is a simple and quick process of embroidery. Because of the fullness involved, soft pliable materials are best. Although there are not many types of stitch used, an unlimited variety of colours and effects can be achieved because of the ways in which they can be combined and adapted. The most common stitches are the outline stitch, the herring-bone, the cable, wave diamond, honeycomb, vandyke and the feathered diamond stitch.

Method
Mark dots at regular intervals of about 6 mm across and down the materials in straight lines. A transfer can be bought, or you can make your own with a piece of card marked at the intervals required and pricked through with a stiletto, so that the point of the pencil can be inserted. Whatever the distance between the dots, the amount of material gathered is usually twice – and sometimes three times – the width wanted in the finished garment.

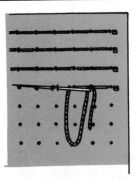

To gather, take a long thread and fasten securely to the right of the first row of dots, then pick up a small piece of material under each dot. When the threads are pulled, the material should fall into regular pleats. Fasten the ends of the threads around pins at the end of the row.

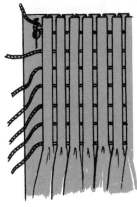

Outline stitch is the basis of most smocking stitches, while *honeycombing* is the most popular stitch. Checked material, especially small two-coloured checks, can be attractive and the checks can be used as a guide for the smocking.

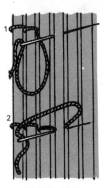

OUTLINE STITCH

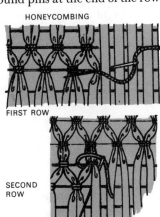

HONEYCOMBING

FIRST ROW

SECOND ROW

Shirring can be gathered by using a large machine stitch and pulling up the threads, or by using elasticated thread in the bobbin with the stitch lengthened and the tension loosened. If shirring is done by hand allow twice the finished width of the material, and to ensure even spacing mark the lines for gathering. Many domestic machines supply an attachment.

Cutting all types of garments

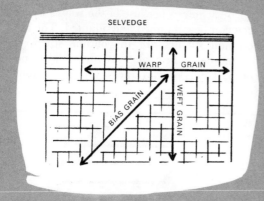

Fundamental rules

Mistakes in cutting can be expensive, but if you remember the fundamental rules about pattern placement you can always avoid them:

1　You should be able to recognise the right and wrong side of the material.
2　Remember that centre fronts and centre backs are usually placed on straight folds or straight threads.
3　The material should be flat and smooth.
4　There should be as little waste as possible.
5　The word 'grain' is used to indicate the direction of threads in the fabric.

The term 'on grain' means that the lengthwise or warp threads cross the crosswise or weft threads at perfect right angles.

'Off grain' means that weft and warp threads cross each other on a slant. Warp threads, lengthwise or selvedge of cloth are usually cut with the fabric going in a vertical direction on the body. Weft threads are more elastic than warp threads and should run evenly across the figure. To ensure accuracy, measure from the selvedge with rulers to be certain each end of the pattern section is the same distance from the edge.

To check the grain pull a weft thread and cut across. If the material is off-grain, grasp the fabric at opposite ends and pull on the bias. If this does not work, try pressing into shape. Warp threads tend to hang straighter when used for gathers and also crease better when used for pleats. Remember always to cut with the grain, press with the grain and sew with the grain.

Brocaded and novelty weaves

Certain brocaded materials are considered reversible, but there are some that are definitely one-way materials. Satin is invariably a one-way fabric, especially in heavier qualities. Many novelty weaves have their designs noticeably surfaced and it is quite easy to distinguish the right or wrong side of such fabrics.

Cutting on the bias

When creating a garment cut on the bias, the designer should bear in mind the difficulties and eliminate as many seams as possible. The bias always drops a considerable amount whether on the true bias or 'off grain' and if skirts are cut on any large pattern section it is

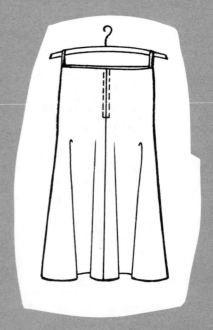

advisable to leave the sections to hang for twenty-four hours before making. This applies especially to skirts to be pleated. Bias material when laid ready for cutting should not be stretched, and should be perfectly flat and smooth. Material is stretched momentarily while it is cut and then shrinks back into its normal size. It is obvious, therefore, that materials must not be stretched when 'laying up', otherwise the garment would be too small when finished.

Precautions needed in cutting garments

1 When the design for the particular fabric has been chosen and the pattern is made, keep the illustration of the style in front of you as you are cutting.

2 Determine the right and wrong side of the cloth.

3 Determine the nap or pile.

4 Examine the grain of the material carefully.

5 Calculate the amount required. Too much or too little means either waste or skimpiness. Work out by experiment the various placings of the pattern pieces for the best arrangement.

6 Plaids and stripes should not be used for a design that is cut up into small pieces.

7 A safe and general rule is to use a fabric of simple design for a garment of a complex pattern design.

8 If using wide fabric, decide whether it is better to open up the fabric for the most economical layout, or to lay the pattern pieces on the double.

9 Narrow material should not be chosen for a design with pattern pieces that are too wide and would require joining.

10 If woollen materials have not been preshrunk, then shrink them first before cutting.

11 Press materials before cutting if they are very creased and straighten the edges.

12 If tearing cloth, be careful that the threads do not pull along the warp and so waste the material.

13 Printed materials which do not have the design on the straight edge need to have the ends cut to follow the design of the cloth.

14 With folded materials, examine the centre fold if the right side is used. Sometimes the fold can be soiled badly and so spoil a layout.

15 When placing patterns place the wider sections first.

16 Do not place the pattern right to the selvedge, but a little further back, so that it can be cut off unless it is particularly desired for a seam turning. If the selvedge is taut, snip to allow it to spread. There are times when the selvedge can be used as a trimming feature.

17 Place all pins in line with the lengthwise grain and pin the material carefully, or clip the material to the table.

18 With silk, chiffons and any fine materials, place paper underneath the layout to prevent slipping and catching in the shears or electric knife.

19 Mark flaws with tailor's chalk so that they are not forgotton (but not on sheer fabrics).

20 When the pieces are all arranged, measure the length over which they extend. Before disturbing them again, it is sometimes advisable to make a rough sketch of the layout in case other garments are required. (This really applies to mass production but it can also be done for a simple layout.)

Velvets

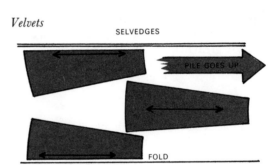

These are usually cut with the pile travelling upwards – that is to say, the material appears darker. This gives a richer appearance to the garment, but many velvets these days can be cut either way. This also applies to corduroys.

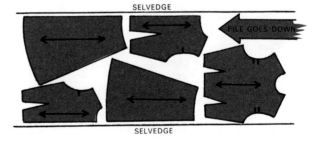

Fabrics with a brushed pile, such as mohair, are cut with the pile downwards.

Cutting sheer fabrics

Chiffon is affected by a moist or damp atmosphere and should always hang for one night before the hem is finished. Unpicking will leave unattractive stitch marks. Pin the material with fine steel pins. If tailor tacks are unsuccessful for marking, trace the markings on to tissue and baste to the wrong side of the fabric. The tissue must be torn away afterwards. If commercial patterns are used, lay the tissue pattern face downwards on the folded sheer fabric. Flip over the fabric and pattern section so that the fabric is face up towards you and all the markings can be clearly seen. Thread-trace the uppermost section of cloth and then take markings through. Never pink the seam edges, otherwise ragged edges will show. Organza, organdie, marquisette, tulle and net hems can be finished with a narrow band of horsehair. Trimmings must be light in weight. Zippers are usually too heavy; buttons, loops, snap fasteners are usually more appropriate. To prevent slipping when sewing, *vanishing muslin* can be used. A tissue toilet roll is also a great help for sewing long seams.

Cutting plaid materials

A simple design with a minimum of seams is best for this material. A small plaid design can be made up in a greater variety of styles, as it is easier to match than large designs.

Types of plaids

There are two kinds of plaids – even and uneven. An even plaid is designed with the pattern exactly the same on both sides of the main bar, and on the lengthwise and crosswise bars. An uneven plaid is not the same on both sides of the outstanding bar of the design. This material can create wastage unless the pattern is designed according to the plaid.

Unbalanced plaid

In an uneven or unbalanced plaid the spaces and colours do not match in both directions. Sometimes the design in a plaid does not form a perfect square. The most successful way to treat an unbalanced plaid is to *match it in one direction around the figure*. The vertical plaid lines will not chevron on the underarm seam on an uneven plaid. The dominant vertical stripe is usually placed down the centre of the garment. The waistline of the bodice and the skirt should be on the same plaid so that there is a regular progression of the plaid from the neck to the hem.

Matching plaid designs throughout the garment

1 To determine whether the plaid is uneven or even, fold the fabric through the centre of any repeat of the design.
2 Small plaids are easier to match than larger ones.
3 For plaids select designs with a minimum number of seams.
4 Avoid circular yokes and many-gored skirts.
5 To determine the extra yardage for plaids, count the number of places in the pattern where the design must be matched and add the plaid design for each location.
6 Mark the plaid on the pattern first before laying out the cloth or pattern.
7 A plaid can only be matched the entire length of a skirt if the side seam edges are identical in degree of slant.
8 When matching the plaid design across the bodice and set-in sleeves, match the plaid at the notches of the sleeve and armhole.
9 It is extremely difficult to match the plaids completely around the armhole because of the curve of the sleeve. If they cannot be matched successfully at both pitches, front and back, match the front bodice and sleeve section to get the most pleasing effect across the whole front of the bodice and armhole.

Stripes

1 Uneven stripes must be cut as you would cut a one-way fabric, with the tops of the pattern pieces all pointing in the same direction.
2 When working with uneven lengthwise stripes and there is no seam at the centre of the bodice and/or skirt, the most harmonious arrangement of the stripes is usually considered to be following right around the figure.

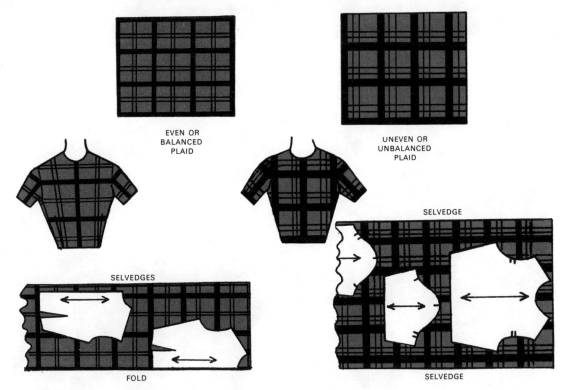

EVEN OR
BALANCED
PLAID

UNEVEN OR
UNBALANCED
PLAID

SELVEDGE

SELVEDGES

FOLD

SELVEDGE

3   When you cut the sleeves of such a pattern, see that the stripes move in the same direction as those in the bodice.
4   If the stripe is required in opposite directions from the centre, plan to have a seam in your pattern at the centre of the bodice and skirt.

Cutting twilled materials

If when you hold the right side of the cloth up towards you, the twill runs from the left shoulder to the right hip, then that is the right side of the twill.

Cutting twills on the bias

Diagonal weaves call for special care in the planning of bias strips and bias seam lines. With twilled materials, you will find that a true bias line, if marked in one direction, will almost follow the lines of the twill, and that the opposite bias will run almost perpendicularly to the twill. Because of this difference between the opposite bias lines, do not use a diagonal weave material for a dress design that requires the use of bias seams. The edges coming together would give an unmatched effect, the diagonal lines running almost at right angles to each other in a decidedly bias seam.

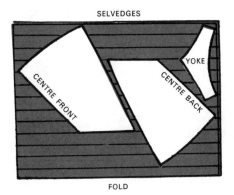

SELVEDGES

CENTRE FRONT

YOKE

CENTRE BACK

FOLD

In a cutting room of a manufacturing firm

Equipment required for cutting

The main item is a cutting room table. This varies according to requirements but it should measure approximately one metre from the floor and the top should be smooth, so that the threads of material do not catch on the board, and broad enough to take cloth one and a half metres in width. The table can be of any length. For wholesale production, the material is opened out flat. For couture work or samples it is sometimes cut on the double. It is an advantage to mark the table in certain dimensions for small lengths.

Clamps should be available for the purpose of securing cloth and marker to the board to prevent slipping (or for single garments, weights can be used). Pins should be at hand for use when cutting small pieces.

For cutting you will need shears or electric knives. For working you will need tailor's chalk. Bags for putting in waste cloth and for collecting the dust from the table will be needed when garment cutting is complete.

Preparing a layout

An economical layout is usually prepared on paper of the same width as the cloth to be used. It is marked in pencil and the pattern sections are laid in the correct grain direction. The pieces of pattern should touch, but not overlap. The selvedge should not be used and allowance for this must be made on the layout. When the layout is finalised a carbon copy of it should be made ready for any other subsequent layouts.

With commercial patterns trim away the surplus paper before placing on the cloth. When the most economical amount of material has been ascertained and duplicates made, these duplicates are called markers and will in turn be laid on the piled lengths, or plies, of cloth.

Where material is very wide and only one garment (or a small number of garments) is required, the layout is often made on the double. The cloth is cut 'on the fold' particularly where stripes and checks are used, as this facilitates the matching of back and front pattern sections and prevents the possibility of a section being omitted. Many high class production firms make miniature layouts or photograph the layouts.

The layout is therefore made according to:

(a) the suitability of the cloth (width, checked, striped etc.)
(b) the usual practice of the firm concerned (whether couture or high class production)
(c) the quantity – whether it is for one garment or one thousand (if for the latter, duplicates or 'markers' are made).

Mechanical aids used in clothing firms

Straight knives

These are used to cut plies several centimetres thick. They can cut out darts and corners easily. There are straight and slot knives, wavy knives for low layouts and notched for heavy fabrics. Knives can have specially cooled blades to prevent fusing on synthetic fabrics. Material should be tested first, as the friction of the blade sometimes causes fusing. The advantages of this knife are the clear unobstructed view of the layout and also the straight cut it provides. Some machines on the market can cut synthetic materials (plastic) without fusing of the material. They have a press-button device which allows a change in speed to whatever is required.

Rotary knives

These have a continuous cut and include band knives. There can be irregularity in cutting if the layout is higher than the middle of the blade. The size of the blade determines the height of the layout. These knives are not suitable for marking notches, owing to the angle of the blade. One advantage of band knives is that they are lighter and easier to handle. The band knife allows two hands to be free. Usually the material is guided to the blade.

Drills

There are various types of drill:

1. Spiral
2. Dye drill
3. Thread drill
4. Hot drill
5. Chalk drill
6. Fluorescent drill
7. Cold drill
8. Hollow drill

Drills must be held at a 90° angle and they are usually portable. They must be tested and set to the correct temperature for each fabric. Fine drills are used for fine cloths and hot drills are used on woven medium-weight cloths. These penetrate and burn a hole to mark the various positions of darts, pockets etc. and are often used to fuse the waste parts of fabric together to prevent slippage. These same drills can be used cold to mark closely woven fabrics. Chalk drills pass through chalk and so mark the fabric. Some drills have a hollow needle and the waste material is disposed of through the hole. Hot drills are used on jersey and woollen goods. They are not, however, used on synthetic materials, as they would fuse the material together.

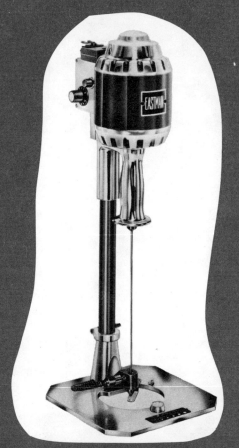

Hot drill

A *hot notcher* is a small machine which notches cloths such as jersey fabrics and woollens and so prevents ravelling from the time they are cut to the time they arrive in the machine room.

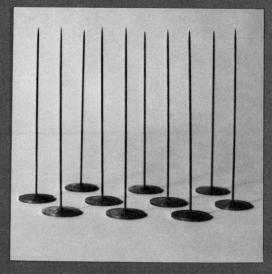

Check spikes are used for accurate positioning of check material when laying up

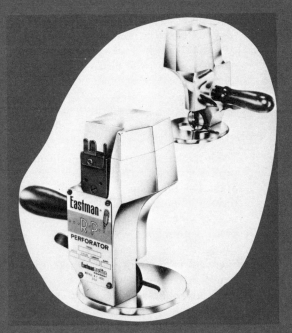

The pattern perforator is a machine which punches evenly spaced perforations on pattern paper. It can be used to make markers.

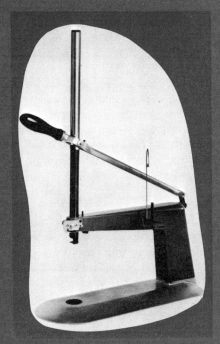

The threadmarker has an adjustable needle rod to penetrate different depths of both natural and synthetic cloths.

The cloth laying machine can be electrically operated and can deal with different widths of cloths. Table clamps automatically catch the folds at the ends of no nap goods. Many automatic cloth spreaders spread napped and patterned goods with plies face-to-face, and the nap or pattern in one direction on all plies.

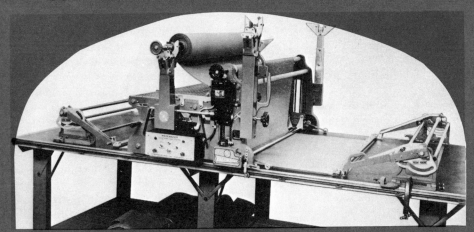

Size combinations

Laying the cloth on the open, or full width, allows better use of the fabric. However, this depends largely upon the various firms and the time factor. Where quantities required in each size are different, or very few, smaller firms find it better to 'lay up' on the double or fold of the cloth. It may be better to make double layouts with one small and one large size garment, or 'scrambled lays' as they say in the trade. It is not possible to use the exact length of cloth, but all firms take into consideration the orders for garments, cloth length, cloth width, cloth availability and how many minutes of labour can be expended in saving 3 cm of material. All this information is gathered together and then the final decisions are made in the cutting rooms. The layouts are made, the markers prepared and then the garments are cut. There is always a percentage of waste, which firms try desperately to avoid, but with woollens the cuttings are very often sold and eventually go back to the mills.

Width of cloth
In many knitwear firms fabric can be knitted to specified widths. Some fabric suppliers will provide the exact width required.

Such an arrangement naturally will depend upon the amount ordered and when making 'markers' the cutter will be able to determine this after his first 'lay'.

Procedure for garment cutting and making in industry

After costing and acceptance the design is sent to the pattern room where:
1 Prototypes are made from the production pattern.
2 They are graded to required sizes.
3 Costings of garments are made (lay making).
4 Markers of layouts are made ready for cutting.
5 Patterns are passed to the stock cutting department, as orders are received.
6 Fabrics are laid up in sizes and materials required and cut in bulk.
7 Garments are bundled and ticketed ready for making.
8 Sewing machine operators sew up the garments.
9 Buttonholes, hems, functional fasteners and trims are applied by trained machinists using specialised machines.
10 Hand-sewing: workers finally attach fasteners, bows, trimmings, etc.

11 Garments are scrutinised for faults or 'passed' by supervisors.
12 After final pressing, the garments go to the department to await dispatch.

Project and Questions

1 From the basic shapes given in the design project make six variations for each style. State the materials you would use, the threads, interfacings and linings. Write details of your method of making and any pressing problems you are likely to encounter.
2 Sketch three different examples of the latest trends in teenage evening wear. Suggest materials suitable for the styles.
3 Sketch two day dresses and suggest the use of two different forms of trimming. The dresses should be suitable for the ready-to-wear market.
4 What special cutting and manufacturing techniques would you use in the cutting of velvets, sheers, and plastic materials?
5 Discuss the uses and types of tapes, stays, edgings, interfacings for quality garment manufacture.
6 How would you indicate faults in fabrics? Give five examples of typical faults. State what should be done to avoid the faults.
7 Twenty questions: Answer yes or no.
   (a) Must the grain line of linings and interfacings always be the same as the main body of the garment? . . . .
   (b) Is an unbalanced plaid wasteful? . . . .
   (c) Would you cut velvet one way? . . . .
   (d) Does 'scye' mean armhole? . . . .
   (e) Does the word 'bridle' apply to tailoring? (See Glossary) . . . .
   (f) In the trade does the term 'bolt' apply to cloth? . . . .
   (g) Can you match stripes at shoulder seams for the entire length of shoulder? . . . .
   (h) Is a line (or ligne) a button measurement? . . . .
   (i) Is the straight knife better for cutting into corners? . . . .

(j) Can a lengthwise edge of plaid be matched to a crosswise edge of plaid when the plaid is an even plaid? ....

(k) When cutting a pattern for a bias skirt would you allow extra on girth? ....

(l) Is it usual to allow the same amount of buttonstand as the diameter of the button? ....

(m) Would you mark the top and bottom button first? ....

(n) Is it better for the pile of camelhair, mohair and velour to run upwards? ....

(o) Is it normal to have easing in the head of a sleeve? ....

(p) Would you use interleaving tissue for cutting? ....

(q) Is the seat angle of a pair of slacks the forepart of the trouser? ....

(r) Is a fly front a concealed opening on a garment? ....

(s) Can plackets be used anywhere on a garment? ....

(t) Is 'bespoke' a tailoring term? ....

Sewing Machines

Selecting a machine

Make yourself familiar with the various types of sewing machine on the market, and buy the one most suitable for your particular needs. It may be a fully automatic compact machine or a plain lockstitch with various attachments. Remember that there is no economy in buying a poor grade machine.

Types of machine

There are three types, the lockstitch, chainstitch and swing needle machines. The automatic is the highest priced, but it is the most versatile and can be used for sewing on buttons, making buttonholes, overlocking raw edges, blind-stitched hems, zigzagging and a great variety of decorative stitches. A book giving full instructions is generally provided with each machine and you should make sure you get one from the dealer or agency. Many agencies give practical instruction in the use of the sewing machine.

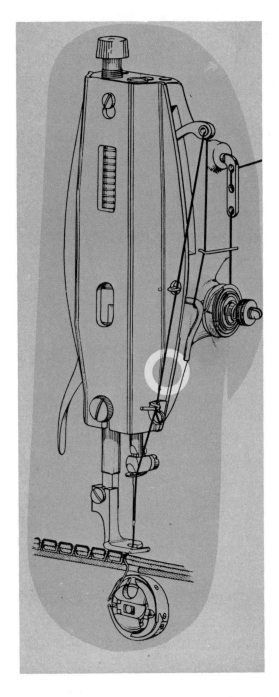

The lockstitch machine uses two threads, an upper and lower, while the chain-stitch uses a single thread (which looks like a lockstitch on the right side, but the thread forms a chain on the underside).

When using an electric machine remember that the speed is regulated by the pressure exerted on the lever. When first practising, press the lever gently to obtain a slow speed until you can achieve an easy regular speed. Slow up gradually as you approach the end of a seam; an abrupt stop jars the mechanism.

Oiling a machine

Drop a very small amount of oil in the places shown in the instructions. Insufficient oil makes the machine run hard; too much may drip on to the material. If the machine is in constant use, oil it sparingly every day and clean it every week.

Care of machines

1 Draw out the work from *behind* the needle. This prevents bending of the needle.
2 Clean the parts near the shuttle with pipe cleaners.
3 Clean fluff from the claw of the footplate or throatplate.
4 Test the tension and size of stitch.
5 Adjust the pressure to the fabrics. (Note the number of turns and turn back the same number afterwards.)
6 Clean the machine for all light-coloured fabrics.
7 When machining armholes or cuffs, machine inside the circles.
8 Use a strong needle to assist the work when turning awkward corners.
9 Always use a needle that corresponds in size to the thread. (Threads that are liable to shrinkage may cause seams to pucker.)
10 Do not pull the fabric.
11 Reduce the speed of the machine when sewing finely woven fabrics.
12 Always keep the slide cover of the bobbin case closed when sewing.

(A Teflon presser foot is invaluable for sewing foamback fabrics or plastic materials.)

Common stitching faults

Looping: Caused by (a) incorrect tension, (b) blunt needle, (c) incorrect threading, (d) bobbin incorrectly threaded, (e) quality of the thread.

Skip stitches: Caused by (a) needle set incorrectly, (b) lack of oil, (c) dirt in claw, (d) needle too fine, (e) needle blunt or bent. If the trouble persists get expert attention.

Upper thread breaking: Caused by (a) wrong needle or incorrect positioning of needle, (b) take-up spring broken, (c) tension discs worn, (d) top tension too tight, (e) needle threaded incorrectly, (f) thread too coarse or poor thread, (g) pressure foot incorrectly adjusted.

Lower thread breaking: Caused by (a) bobbin wound too tightly, (b) unevenly wound bobbin, (c) bobbin too full, (d) worn spring on bobbin, (e) bobbin incorrectly threaded.

Pulled threads: Caused by a blunt needle.

Puckers in stitching: Caused by (a) tight tension, (b) incorrect threading of upper thread, (c) too much or too little pressure on pressure foot.

Machine attachments

It is essential to know how to work the various attachments on a machine. The binder, hemmer, tucker, cording foot, ruffler, hemstitcher, darner, etc. all assist in turning out professional-looking results. The instruction books give details of all the attachments but an hour's lesson from a demonstrator at a sewing centre is much better than many pages of written instructions.

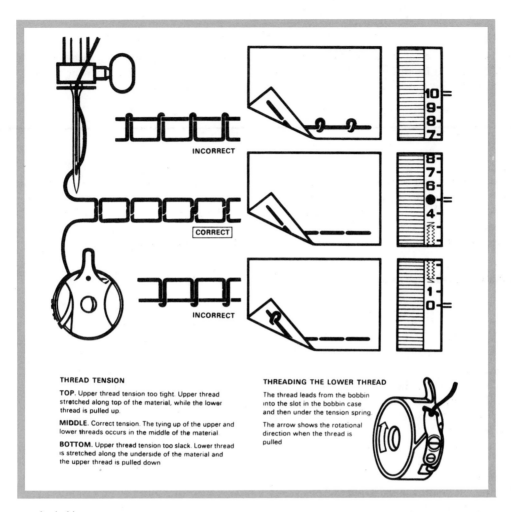

THREAD TENSION

TOP. Upper thread tension too tight. Upper thread stretched along top of the material, while the lower thread is pulled up.

MIDDLE. Correct tension. The tying up of the upper and lower threads occurs in the middle of the material.

BOTTOM. Upper thread tension too slack. Lower thread is stretched along the underside of the material and the upper thread is pulled down

THREADING THE LOWER THREAD

The thread leads from the bobbin into the slot in the bobbin case and then under the tension spring.

The arrow shows the rotational direction when the thread is pulled

Ornamental stitching

Ornamental stitching can be produced by many of the latest machines, but for people who do not have a modern machine this type of stitching can be achieved by winding the bobbin with embroidery silk and using the normal sewing thread in the needle. The upper tension should be loosened slightly, while the under tension should be entirely released, so that the thicker silk may pull freely from the bobbin. Proceed as for ordinary sewing, but with the right side of the material face down; the design should be marked on the wrong side. The length of stitch should vary according to the design, and the machine should be run slowly. Many different effects can be achieved by using coloured threads, by altering the length of the stitch and by running rows of vertical lines and contrasting horizontal lines to create novel patterns. For people who like embroidery, there are very few hand embroidery stitches that cannot be replaced by the sewing machine of today.

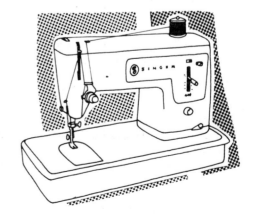

Final advice

Always have spare needles available. Cover the machine when it is not in use. Clean and oil it regularly. In this way you will have very little trouble with tension and bad stitching. It is neglect of the mechanism which causes many machine troubles.

Needle sizes

To do a proper job of work the needles used must be suited to the thread and the material. The type of machine you have will determine the type of needle you buy. Needles such as Milward's will fit many popular sewing machines, but it is as well to consult your instruction book before buying. A good quality needle is advisable, as inferior brands may have a blunt point or sharp eye which may fray the thread. This also applies to hand needles.

Needle and thread size chart

	Threads		Needles Domestic machine needles		Hand
Fine fabrics: Nylon, Terylene, Satin, Lawn, Silk, Chiffon, Organdie, Lace *N.B. Use thicker needles and threads for heavier lace*	Perivale Polyester 100	Coats Super Sheen 50 or Gossamer	Continental 60–70	Singer 9–11	9–11
Medium fabrics: Cotton, Poplin, Linen, Dress wool, Synthetic blends	100	50–40	70–90	11–14	8–9
Blends			80–90	12–14	7–8
Fine suitings	100	40	80–90	12–14	7–8
Fine corduroy	100	40	80–90	12–14	7–8
Jersey fabrics	100	40	80–90	12–14	7–8
Plastic materials	100	40	80–90	12–14	7–8
Open weaves and laminates	100	40	80–90	12–14	7–8
Medium worsteds	100	40	80–90	12–14	7–8
N.B. Needles and threads will vary for jersey depending on whether it is silk or wool					
Heavy fabrics: Worsteds	100	40	90–100	14–16	7–8
Denim, Tweed, Heavy furnishings,	30 twist	24	100–110	16–18	6–5
Coatings	30 twist	24	100–110	16–18	6–5
Canvas, Duck, Ticking	30 twist	chain-stitch 10	110–120	18–20	4

Remember that the seams of jersey garments should be taped to prevent stretching. Tape seams for laminates also. Please note: the higher the thread number, the finer it is.

When changing from cotton to synthetic threads you may find it necessary to change to a finer needle size. Synthetic threads are stronger than cotton of the same thicknesses. Consequently a synthetic thread producing a seam of a particular strength would be finer than cotton used for the same purpose. Success in sewing depends very much upon using the correct thread and needle size. If the needle is too small, the thread cannot pass easily through the eye. The result is fraying and weak seams, and breaking of the thread.

It is advisable to consult your sewing machine guide instructions for further details about threads and needles.

For industrial machines the following firms have their own thread advisory services:

J. & P. Coats Ltd.	50 Bothwell Street, Glasgow C.2
English Sewing Ltd.	56 Oxford Street, Manchester 1
Sewing Silks Ltd.	Perivale Mills, Greenford, Middlesex.

Before garments are made all materials should be tested for suitability of thread, and stitch-length while the machine should be adjusted for pressure and tension.

Sewing threads
Cotton threads withstand high temperatures, pressing and needle heating better than synthetic threads.

Synthetic threads, because of their low shrinkage properties, do not pucker in wash-and-wear garments or in dry-cleaning.

Silk threads, mostly used for buttonholes and edge-stitching in tailored garments and for decorative embroidery in light clothing, always have a good appearance, although the threads do not have the strength and abrasion resistance of the synthetics.

Fitting

Fitting principles

A garment can be considered to fit well when all its basic construction lines assume normal positions on the body. There must be no restriction of movement, but at the same time there must be no unnecessary wrinkles and folds. There should be no appearance of tightness or dragging on any part of the body.

The garment should feel easy and comfortable and the proportion and styling should be taken into account during the fitting process. Side seams must be straight and in line with the shoulder seam (depending, of course, on the design). A skirt should hang straight down from the hip line and should allow enough ease for sitting comfortably. There should be a basting thread down the centre front and the centre back, so that you can see immediately whether the garment is balanced properly.

Personal preferences
If someone requires a close-fitting garment, then one can only comply with the request, even though it may not be best for the individual concerned. A great deal depends upon the stature and proportions of the person. Try in the fitting procedure to play down any major figure faults with people who are not standard size. In many instances current fashion may be ignored to suit the customer's requirements and peculiarities of fit.

General procedure

Give confidence at the fitting by appearing efficient and methodical. Ask the person to be fitted, in a polite way, to stand naturally and ask whether she is wearing normal foundation garments. The dress is usually fitted with the right side out to give the wearer a true perspective of the garment at this stage.

1 Check the balance of the garment by seeing that the grain hangs naturally at the centre front and centre back and is not distorted in any way. The weft should be kept horizontal across the bust line.

2 Deal with one seam at a time, but begin with the shoulder, seeing that there is no drag or pull in that area. Stroke and smooth any wrinkles towards the shoulder line and re-pin if necessary.

3 Check that the side seams hang straight from underarm to hemline.

4 Owing to the differences in habitual posture, some areas may be more muscular than others. This will entail fitting both sides of the body.

5 If the armholes appear tight, allow more room and be sure to ask if there is discomfort anywhere.

6 Check the bust point position and fit under the bust, easily yet cleanly.

7 Mark the waistline clearly and keep the grain straight on the bust while correcting the waistline.

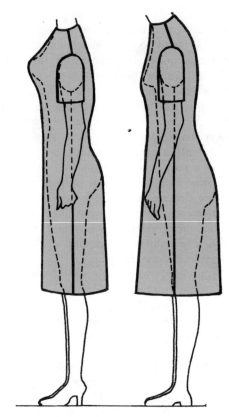

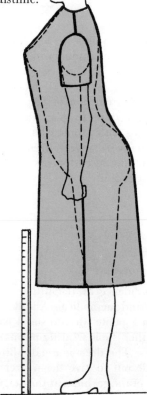

8 The length of the garment is generally regulated from the ground. A metre stick and chalk is usual. It is an advantage to the fitter if the person being fitted stands on a table or platform.

9 Run a gathering thread round the top of the sleeve about 1 cm from the edge. Slip the sleeve on the arm and see that the straight grain of the fabric runs in a vertical line from the top of the armhole.

10 When fitting skirts have the waistband made, marking the centre front and centre back of the band. Pin the centre front and centre back of the skirt to the band as it would be when worn.

All alterations must be clearly marked before taking off the garment. Any special comments should be noted and referred to when re-cutting, especially for peculiarities of the figure.

Correct the garment immediately; otherwise it is so easy to forget minor details and marks (especially chalk) can sometimes disappear. Make notes of any special points you wish to remember or discuss with the customer.

Garment construction

After the fitting process

The making procedure, both for a production garment and an individual garment, will depend greatly upon the style and the fabric used. However, the quickest and easiest method of construction for a dress is the following, provided the opening is at the centre back or the centre front.

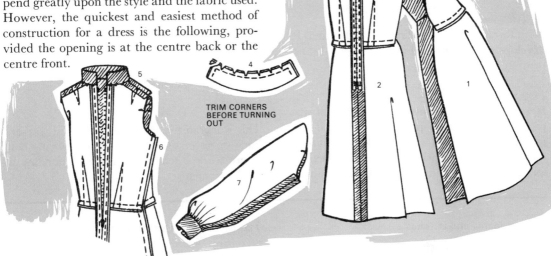

TRIM CORNERS
BEFORE TURNING
OUT

Sewing sequence

1 Complete the stitching of all darts, seams or trimming features on the front and insert the zip, if the design specifies this.
2 Complete the stitching of all seams and darts on the back and insertion of the zip, if the design specifies this.
3 Join the front and back together at the shoulders.
4 Make the collar if required.

5 Apply the collar to the neck edge, or neaten the neck edge with a facing, or any other desired finish.
6 Join the underarm seams.
7 Make the sleeves, adding and finishing the cuff if need be.
8 Attach the sleeve to the main garment.
9 Finish the hem. Make the buttonholes. Sew on the buttons, press studs or hooks and eyes.
10 Complete with the final pressing.

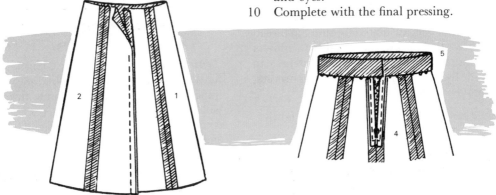

Skirt construction

1 Complete the skirt front.
2 Complete the skirt back.
3 Join the front and back together.

4 Insert the zip or complete opening.
5 Apply the skirt band.
6 Turn and finish the hem. Complete with the final pressing.

Production methods of making up garments

Make through
This method means that a garment can be made on the flat or on the dress stand. It is used in couture houses or small firms.

Semi-divisional
With this method young labour can be used. It develops team spirit and is used by small and medium class firms.

Progressive bundle system
Here bundles of garments (unsorted) of approximately twenty parts are stitched by machinists and then returned to the bundle ready for the next girl. This system is flexible for different styles and medium skill is required.

However, parts can be lost and the tying and untying is time-consuming. Bundles are passed to the next operator either by a chute or by being pushed along a table.

Synchro Flo
Semi-skilled labour is suitable here. Garments and sections progress automatically, tilt tables are used, but a large output of work is necessary to make the system economic.

Straight line conveyor
This works to the speed of the slowest worker. Each operator sits at the side of a moving belt where work is fed to her in small bundles or single garments.

Various seams and stitches

The old rule of 'pin before you tack, tack before you sew', is vital for beginners. An experienced machinist pins and takes the pins out as she sews. She depends upon the notches and balance marks to guide her. However, until you have considerable experience, the old rule still applies.

Temporary stitches
These are used to hold the material in place in preparation for fitting. Knots are used for fastening, but should be on the outside for easy removal. Unnecessary threads should be removed before stitching. When withdrawing threads from delicate materials, snip the thread every few stitches; otherwise pulling a thread may tear the material. Temporary stitches can be made by machine for experimental purposes, but use the largest stitch.

Slanted basting: This is used for slippery fabric.

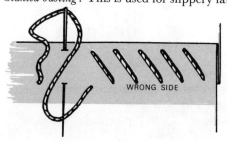

Tacking stitches: Even stitches are used when preparing for machining. Long stitches are used for seams with little strain. A combination of long and short stitches is used for finer materials.

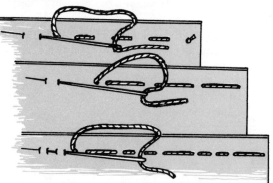

Tailor tacking or mark stitching: This is used to mark-stitch the location of darts, pleats, trimmings etc. Use a coloured double thread that will show readily. Take either one or two stitches through the double cloth and leave long ends. Pull the cloth open and snip through the tacks.

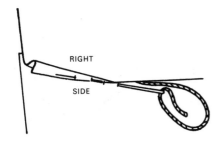

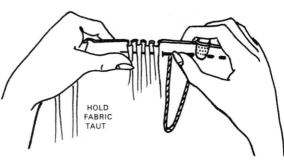

Slip tacking: This stitch is for making alterations on the right side of materials. It is used for sheer fabrics and in the fitting process.

Running stitches: These will hold two pieces of cloth together and will gather fabric very quickly. Hold the fabric taut. Hold the needle as you hold a pencil with the first finger behind the cloth. Wiggle the needle up and down through the fabric until the needle is full of stitches, then push them back on to the thread.

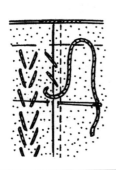

Padding stitches: These are used in tailoring for collars and revers, to hold the canvas to the main body of the garment.

Seams

The plain seam is most generally used in sewing. The inside finish is determined by the weave and the texture of the cloth.

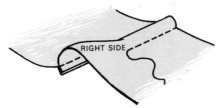

French seam: This type of seam is used a great deal for lingerie and all fine and sheer fabrics where the raw edges need to be concealed.

Lapped seam: This is used on tailored garments, yokes or even in the waistline of garments. It can be used over gatherings. If cut on a concave curve the seams must be notched where required.

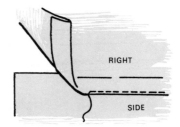

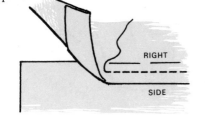

Tucked seam: This seam can be attractive as a decorative feature, but is not suitable for very thick materials.

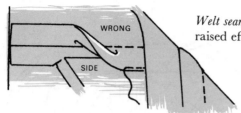

Welt seam: This is used for thick materials and raised effects.

Run and fell seam: This seam is used for garments which will be subject to hard wear and also for sheer fabrics.

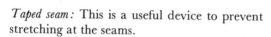

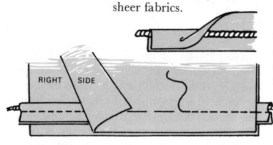

Corded seam: This is used in home decoration for cushions and loose covers and is often used with gathering on garments or as a trimming feature, for example in the waistline of dresses.

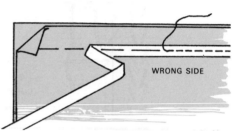

Taped seam: This is a useful device to prevent stretching at the seams.

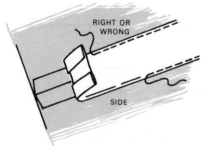

Strap seam: This seam is decorative and contrasts can be used.

Slot seam: This is another decorative seam, used on medium-weight cloths.

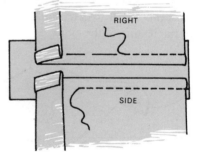

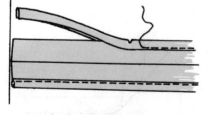

Bound seam: Thick materials which fray easily can be bound at the seam with self or contrast material or a thin bias silk.

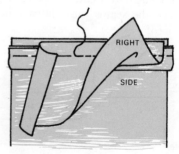

Piped seam: This is used to accentuate a plain seam by a contrast in colour or it can be used as a trimming with a different material.

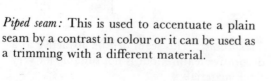

Hand stitches

Joining two edges together

1 Diagonal overcasting – used for joining felted materials.

2 Running stitches. Zig-zag for darning worn sections.

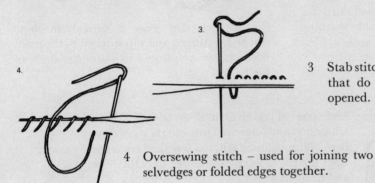

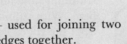

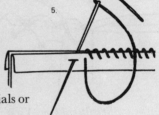

3 Stab stitch – used on felt materials or cloths that do not fray, then pressed flat and opened.

4 Oversewing stitch – used for joining two selvedges or folded edges together.

5 Whipping stitch – used for fine materials or on seams that fray.

General work

1 Back stitch, strengthening stitch.

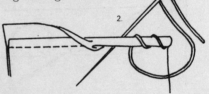

2 Overcasting – for material which frays easily. The edge can be rolled and overcast.

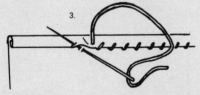

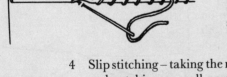

3 Plain hemming stitches – used on folded edge and narrow hems. The stitches are small.

4 Slip stitching – taking the needle along hem and catching a small portion on the main parts.

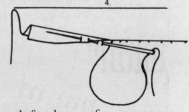

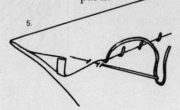

5 Vertical hemming – used for hems of dresses. It is spaced further apart than plain hemming.

Skirt hem finishes

Skirt hems can be wide or narrow, depending upon the design and texture of the fabric. Straight skirts usually have a 5 cm or 6 cm hem. For flared and circular skirts the hems are narrow. Facings are usual for shaped and scalloped hemlines, and with thick materials the edges can be bound or finished with a tape or pre-shrunk binding. Circular pleated skirts are usually either hemstitched or double machine stitched. Hems can be finished with ruffles, braiding, pleating, piping or ribbon.

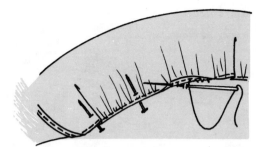

Circular hem: The edge is turned, machine stitched, gathered and slip stitched to the main body. It can be pleated to follow the curve of the hem.

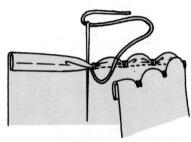

Shell hem: This gives a decorative finish to trimmings and lingerie. Turn and tack a narrow hem. With running stitches sew the hem 5 cm from the edge. Take two stitches over the edge and draw tight.

Slip-stitched hem: First machine stitch 5 cm from the edge. Turn and pin the hem. Slip the needle between the stitched edge and catch lightly to the cloth.

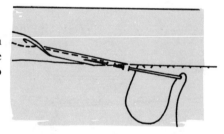

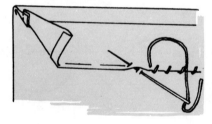

Faced hem: This is used for thick fabrics. A thin self-colour material is used and machined on to a turned narrow hem. It is tacked and either herringboned, hemmed or slip-stitched.

Bonded hem: Sheer materials can be treated in this way. The hem material has adhesive on both sides. It is cut and bonded on to the cloth with a warm iron. The edge can be neatened, left raw or overlocked.

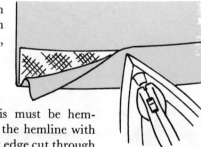

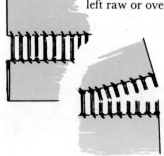

Picot or hemstitched edge: This must be hemstitched by specialists. Mark the hemline with self-colour thread. For a picot edge cut through the centre of the hemstitching.

Horsehair hem: Narrow horsehair is machined to the hem and then hand-stitched. This method is for sheer fabrics.

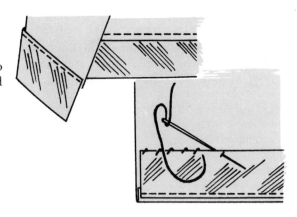

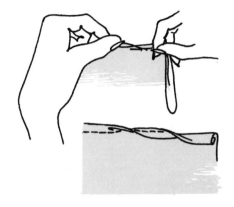

Stitched and rolled hem: This is used on sheer fabrics. Roll the edge between the thumb and forefinger and catch the roll in position with hemming stitches.

Seam finishes

The different ways of finishing seams will depend on the fabric and the purpose of the garment.

Overlock seam: A quick method of finishing lightweight materials.

Overcast seam: For heavier materials that ravel.

Neatened seam: For light materials where a firmer and stronger edge is required. The raw edges are turned towards the seam line and pressed open.

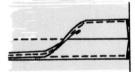

Turned edges stitched together: Used on underwear or outer garments of lightweight fabrics. (Stitch an ordinary seam, turn the raw edges towards seam and stitch together, press to one side.)

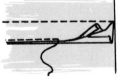

Rolled seam: Used for sheer fabrics. Stitch a plain seam, then roll the seam between thumb and forefinger and overcast close to the stitching.

Bound seam: For unlined jackets and coats. Encase each edge with bias or pre-shrunk tape. Tack and machine stitch through all the thicknesses.

Darts and tucks

Darts are used to dispose of fullness and to give a good fit to the garment. They are generally pressed towards the centre back and centre front of the garment. On the sleeve they are usually pressed towards the wrist on the elbow. Darts must not extend beyond the point of the bust, elbow, hip or any bulge, and they should taper to a thread – otherwise a pleat will be formed. They can be slit and pressed open and can also be used as decorative features.

Dart: Mark the dart with tailor's chalk, pins or tacks. Fold the fabric between the markings in a straight line to a point. Stitch from the edge to the point. Heavy fabric and deep darts require slashing through the centre.

Body dart: This is used at the waistline. Taper to a thread, press and slit to allow the dart to spread.

Dart tuck: The fullness is released within the garment. Stitch as for an ordinary dart. Machine across after pressing for an inverted pleat, through dart thickness only.

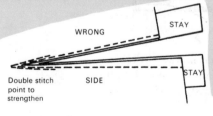

Slashed dart with stay: Place a stay on the right side. Machine along the dart markings through the fabric and stay. Slash between the stitchings and turn the stay to the inside. Tack flat at the edge. Pull gathers to fit the shorter section. Tack and stitch inside or outside. Outside stitches tend to strengthen the point.

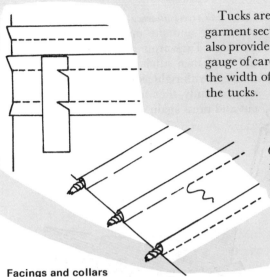

Tucks are a means of bringing fullness into a garment section where it is needed and they can also provide decoration. Always use a measuring gauge of cardboard for tucks, and notch to show the width of the tuck and the distance between the tucks.

Corded tucks: These can be done by hand or machine. Fit a special cording foot after tacking the cord in position if using a machine.

Facings and collars

There are three kinds of facing, the shaped, the extended and the bias. They are cut to finish an edge and are usually separate pieces of material on the inside of the garment, although for decorative purposes they can be cut and stitched to fall on the outside of the garment.

Shaped facings are usually cut to the shape of armholes, necklines, hems and yokes.

Extended facings are cut in one with front and back openings, on the bodice or skirt, straight collars and cuffs and sleeve openings.

Bias facings are usually narrow bias strips of materials to finish the edges of hems, collars, necklines and sleeve edges.

Facings can be joined to collars first and then attached to the main garment. They should be caught down at the cross seams with a loose stitch, or if the material is springy the facing can be stitched into the seam (from the right side). This is known as *sink stitching*. If carefully done it blends in with the seam.

Attach facings to plain necklines and trim to within 6 mm of the sewing line. Then open out the facing and turn the seam allowances under the facing. On the wrong side of the material stitch very close to the seam through all thicknesses of the cloth on the facing side of the seam. In this way you will find that when the seam is pressed back the facing rolls over neatly.

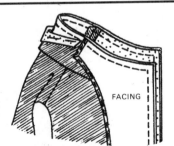

Collar inserted between facing Make up the collar by joining the under-collar to the top-collar, easing the top to the under section. The interfacing is usually cut as the top-collar in dressmaking. Trim away the excess seam allowance. Snip off the points of the corners and turn inside out, then tack if necessary but endeavour to

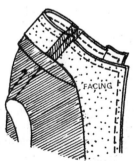

finger press and then press with a hot iron and steam if required. Insert the collar between main body of the garment and the facing and stitch carefully. Fold the facing back and press.

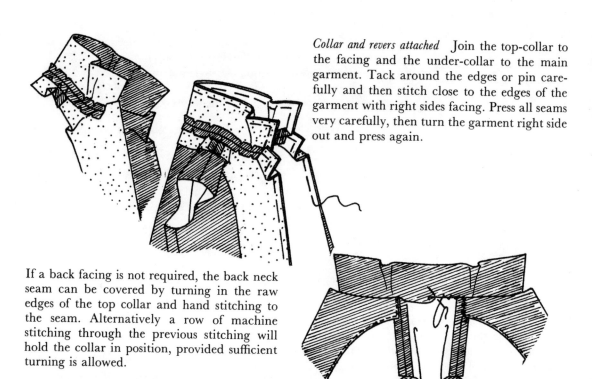

Collar and revers attached Join the top-collar to the facing and the under-collar to the main garment. Tack around the edges or pin carefully and then stitch close to the edges of the garment with right sides facing. Press all seams very carefully, then turn the garment right side out and press again.

If a back facing is not required, the back neck seam can be covered by turning in the raw edges of the top collar and hand stitching to the seam. Alternatively a row of machine stitching through the previous stitching will hold the collar in position, provided sufficient turning is allowed.

Cuffs and plackets

Cuffs must be designed to suit the sleeve on which they are being used. They can be cut in one with the sleeve or separately; if cut separately they may consist of one piece of material on the fold, or of two pieces seamed and joined together. Interfacing is usual where crispness is required or where there is a button and button-stand.

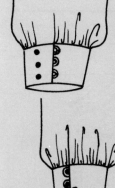

Fold-over cuff If the sleeve is wide enough to pull over the hand then no opening is required. Buttonhole loops are made and inserted into the seamline of the cuff and the buttons are sewn on the cuff to match. This method can apply to a sleeve without a cuff. Another method is to make a tight cuff, leaving a gap of approximately 5 to 6 cm on the under side of the sleeve and finishing with a small hem.

Small hem on wrong side at gap.

Band-edge cuff Stitch the right side of the cuff to the right side of the sleeve. Turn to the wrong side, folding to the width desired, and catch back the turned-in edge to the seam. Another simple method with thin material is to make up the cuff and attach to the sleeve, laying the right sides together. Overlock or neaten all the raw edges.

Frilled cuff Turn up a hem sufficiently deep to allow 3 cm for the frill and neaten the raw edges. Approximately 6 cm should be sufficient for the turnings, the width of stitching and neatening. If a drawstring is used a small buttonhole should be made in the approximate position.

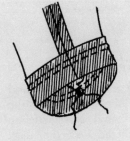

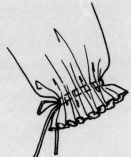

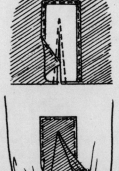

Plain cuff Make a slit in the sleeve 8 to 9 cm long. Face it with a piece of material approximately 12 cm long and 6 to 7 cm wide. Machine within 5 mm of the slit. Nick into the corner and turn to the wrong side. Gather the lower edge of the sleeve and attach the cuff, laying the right side of the cuff and sleeve together. The gathering should be even on the sleeve, and allowance made on the cuff for the button and buttonhole. The cuff is folded over and the point stitched, then turned inside out. The cuff is neatened inside either by hand or by machine.

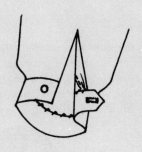

Plackets Plackets are openings in any part of the garment and can be found in necklines of bodices or skirts. They are often placed in seams, but can be cut as a slash in the fabric. They can be closed at one or both ends of a garment, they can be faced, bound or 'grown on'.

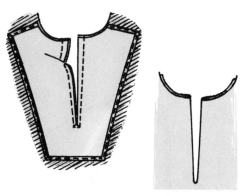

Placket in seam The seam allowances can be used as part of the facing. At the end of the opening clip through the seam allowance on one side only. Press the seam open. Neaten the edges by binding or by bias strips. Many openings, especially on sleeves, can be 'grown on', the seam allowances being extended at particular points.

Faced opening If faced on the right side this may be used as a decoration. Cut the facing on the fold and make a crease to define the centre. Place the right sides together over the line of the opening. Machine around the marked opening, making two small stitches at the point. Cut and nick into the point, turn the facing inside, press the edge and edge-stitch either inside or outside as a decoration.

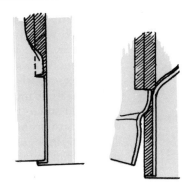

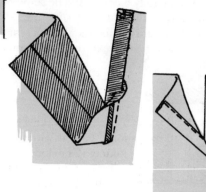

Bound opening To make a continuous bound slash, cut a strip of material twice as long as the slit. Cut the required width and crease to define the centre. Place the right sides together with the strip underneath as you machine. Keep the seam even on the binding, but on the garment taper the seam to a point at the end of the slit. Turn under and top-stitch over the seam.

Sleeves

In the main the same method of applying can be used for the majority of sleeve types, whether they are set high or low on the shoulder. Sleeves should, when finished, have no drag or pull and no strain around the head of the sleeve.

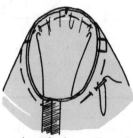

One-piece sleeve Attach the cuffs and finish the sleeve ready for setting into the bodice. Gather the sleeve head, or machine the darts if there is a darted top, turn the sleeve to the outside and the garment to the inside, so that the right sides are together. Begin pinning the sleeve into the armhole by first putting underarm seams together, matching notches and easing in the surplus in the sleeve head. Never stretch the bodice to match the sleeve. Tack carefully, again from the underarm, then machine-stitch from the sleeve side. Remove the tacking stitches. First press open the seam and afterwards press all the seams towards the sleeve to give extra body in the sleeve head.

Two-piece sleeves These sleeves usually have canvas at the wrist, and are inserted in the same way as the one-piece sleeve, except that the two seams are either side of the side seam of the bodice.

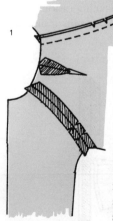

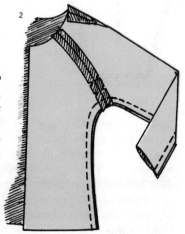

Raglan sleeves These are cut either in one or two sections. If a dart is used instead of a seam, stitch it carefully, open and press it flat. If the sleeve is cut with a seam, match the notches and put the easing where required. It is usual to match the front and back bodice sections to the sleeve and stitch them, afterwards clipping at the underarm seams so that they can be pressed flat. Then pin the underarm seams together and stitch the full length of the underarm and sleeve seam.

Magyar sleeves Many people call these 'kimono with a gusset', but in the trade people often refer to them as magyar-type sleeves.

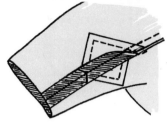

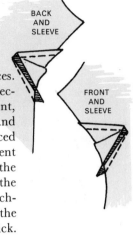

BACK AND SLEEVE

FRONT AND SLEEVE

The gussets can be cut in one or two pieces. It is easier for insertion if they are in two sections. Cut the slash to within 4 mm of the point, laying the right sides of both garment and gusset together. (The point can be reinforced first, while the slash is usually stitched to prevent fraying.) Stitch very carefully towards the point, allowing two stitches actually at the point, before turning. A retaining row of stitching may be made. Gussets are usually on the bias and may be lined if the main cloth is thick.

The kimono sleeve The underarm of this sleeve can be reinforced after pressing and clipping the seam allowance by applying a strip of bias tape or binding laid flat on the opened seam. A row of top stitching at each side of the seam need not be obvious. Another method is to apply a tape as the seam is stitched.

Shoulder pads (for washable dresses) Cut two crescents of dress fabric approximately 14 cm long and 8 cm deep and insert washable nylon padding between them, graduating the amount towards the curve. Tack and stitch. If a larger pad is wanted several thicknesses of nylon wadding can be inserted between two triangles, or a square may be cut and folded in half. For puffed sleeves several squares of self fabric (cut then folded over to form a triangle and the material stepped towards the point) can be stitched to form firm pads. Pads should be placed with the pointed end in the centre of the shoulder so that the thick part extends over the shoulder point.

Pockets

Pockets may be placed in any position. They can be completely functional or used as a decorative feature. There are several types of

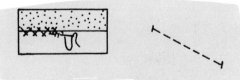

Note: The welt pocket may be machine or hand-stitched, according to the type of garment.

pocket and many different styles are possible with the use of all kinds of trimming. The most popular types are the welt, patch, jetted and flap pockets.

Welt pocket Cut the welt the length and width required. An average length for an adult is approximately 16 cm for dresses and a little more for coats and suits. Allow seam turnings on the welt and cut on the fold. The interfacing is usually single. Mark the position of the opening.

143

Welt pocket (continued)

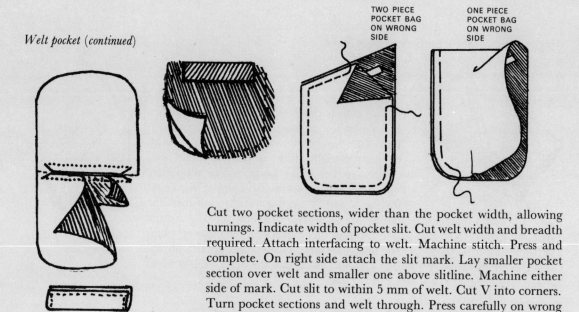

TWO PIECE POCKET BAG ON WRONG SIDE

ONE PIECE POCKET BAG ON WRONG SIDE

Cut two pocket sections, wider than the pocket width, allowing turnings. Indicate width of pocket slit. Cut welt width and breadth required. Attach interfacing to welt. Machine stitch. Press and complete. On right side attach the slit mark. Lay smaller pocket section over welt and smaller one above slitline. Machine either side of mark. Cut slit to within 5 mm of welt. Cut V into corners. Turn pocket sections and welt through. Press carefully on wrong side. Machine pocket sections together.

Jetted pocket   This is similar to a piped button-hole. Mark the position of the opening. Cut two strips 4 cm longer than the width of the pocket and 3 cm wide for a narrow piping. Cut two pocket linings, one longer than the other. Fold the strips in half lengthwise and lay them on the right side of the garment, raw edges to the marked position. Lay the pocket pieces on top, and machine 6 mm either side of the slit for length of pocket opening.

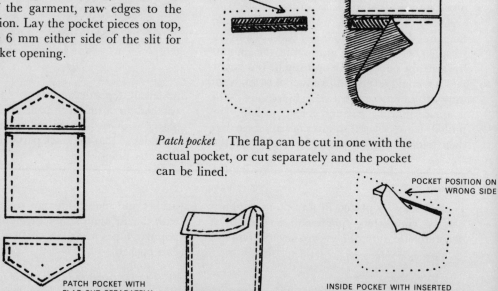

POCKET PIECES LAID OVER PIPING STRIPS ON RIGHT SIDE

POCKET BAG POSITION ON WRONG SIDE

Patch pocket   The flap can be cut in one with the actual pocket, or cut separately and the pocket can be lined.

POCKET POSITION ON WRONG SIDE

PATCH POCKET WITH FLAP CUT SEPARATELY

INSIDE POCKET WITH INSERTED FLAP AND PIPED POCKET OPENING

Buttonholes

Buttons and buttonholes are both decorative and functional. There are three types of button-hole, the handworked one, the bound button-hole and the loop buttonhole. First mark the position and size of the buttonhole. The buttonhole should be 3 mm longer than the button for a 40-line (or 2·5 cm diameter) button. The amount over and above the button width will vary according to the size of the button. A buttonhole should never be made too tight so that a button is forced through a hole. Whatever allowance has been made for the button, it is usually placed in the centre of the under part of the opening. A buttonstand is the part from the button to the edge of the opening and is often the width or diameter of the button.

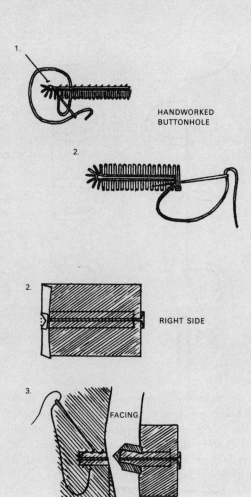

HANDWORKED BUTTONHOLE

RIGHT SIDE

FACING

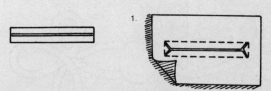

Bound buttonhole Cut two strips 3 cm longer than the buttonhole and 5 cm wide. Place the centre of the strip to the buttonhole with right sides facing. Stitch 3 mm either side of the basting line of the buttonhole and across the ends. Slash on the line to within 6 mm of ends and then cut diagonally to the corners. Turn the strip to the inside, turning the seams away from the opening. Make an inverted pleat at the ends forming a piping on the outside with the edges meeting at the centre of the buttonhole. Pull out the triangle ends to stitch to the piping. Neaten the edges as invisibly as possible.

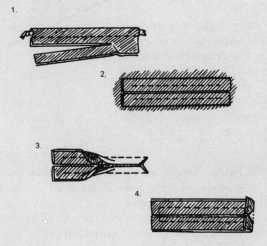

Piped buttonhole Cut sufficient bias (approximately 2 cm wide) for all the buttonholes and fold lengthwise. Insert cord if required. Trim the raw edges to 3 mm after machining, then cut two straight strips each 2 cm longer than the buttonhole. On the right side of the garment place the strips with the raw edges meeting, on the line of the buttonhole. Stitch 3 mm either side of the centre for length of buttonhole. On wrong sides slash to within 6 mm of the ends and clip into the corners. Turn the pipings to the inside and then stitch the triangular ends to the piping. The facing when turned and cut should be neatly stitched.

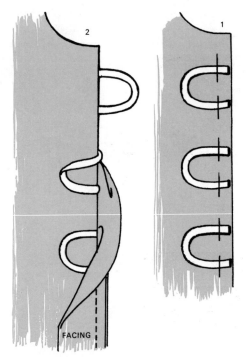

Loop buttonholes Loops can be worked by hand by making a bar and then buttonhole-stitching over the bar, or piped loops can be made and inserted into a seam. They can be filled with cord or a round braid. Apply the loops before attaching the facing. Sometimes they are applied to paper first and then stitched to the garment; this will depend upon the type of material. Cut all the loops to the same length and see that they are evenly spaced, and facing away from the edge, as illustrated. The paper is torn away after stitching.

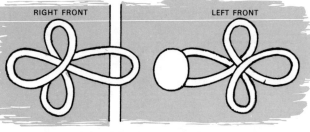

Sewing buttons Start by three small back stitches on the wrong side of the button position. If the material is thick place a pin or match stalk under the button and then bind the threads by winding round the sewing thread. A buttonhole stitch is sometimes used.

Decorative button loops Sometimes called frogs, these are made from rouleaux, narrow bias strips machined and then turned inside out. It is advisable to draw the outline first on brown paper, shaping the frog right side down so that the seams are uppermost as the design is made.

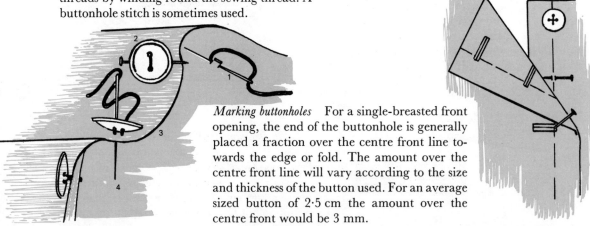

Marking buttonholes For a single-breasted front opening, the end of the buttonhole is generally placed a fraction over the centre front line towards the edge or fold. The amount over the centre front line will vary according to the size and thickness of the button used. For an average sized button of 2·5 cm the amount over the centre front would be 3 mm.

Zips

There are many types of zips made to suit all materials and designs. The invisible zipper is one which disappears into the opening of the garment and cannot be seen from the outside. The metal zipper is used on materials of thicker and harder textures. The nylon zipper is for lighter weight materials, but requires careful checking of the iron temperature if it is pressed. The open-end zipper is used on many weights of cloth for cardigans, jackets, and all garments requiring an opening top and bottom.

There are several ways of inserting the zips.

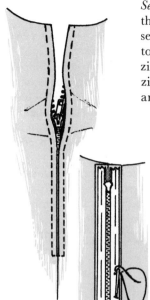

Semi-concealed or half-and-half First complete the seam to the point where the zip is to be inserted, and using a very large stitch and looser top tension continue stitching to the required zip length. Press the seam open. Change to a zipper foot. (There are two kinds, the plain one and the hinged foot.)

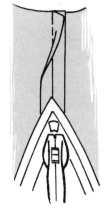

Place the zip fastener face down on the wrong side of the seam. Tack and follow the instructions on the zip packet about the amount to allow from the coils to the stitching line. Stitch either side of the zip and finally remove the tacking stitches down the centre of the seam line, so that the zip is exposed. For necklines it is advisable not to stitch the zip to the top but to leave a small space for a hook and eye to be attached. A zip shield is usually cut and attached to better-class garments. This is a strip of material the length (plus approximately 3 cm) of the zip and approximately 6 cm wide, neatened to prevent the zip coils catching in undergarments.

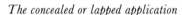

The concealed or lapped application
With this method one side of the opening forms a lap over the zip, completely concealing it, although it requires good seam allowances – a minimum of 2 cm. Bias binding can be stitched to the seams to extend them. The finished appearance is neat with one row of visible stitching while the lap provides ample coverage for the zip. It is best on light and medium-weight fabrics. Remember to use the zipper foot because it is extremely difficult to stitch close enough to the teeth without one.

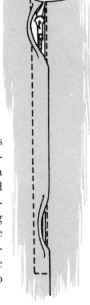

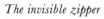

The invisible zipper
Before attaching the collar, waistband or facing the zip should be applied, and even before the remainder of the seam is stitched. Tack the seam together and press open. With the zipper teeth uppermost tack the tape to the seam turnings only. Remove tackings in the seam and fully open the zip. With the zipper foot stitch close to the coil, keeping the teeth uppermost. In the same way, stitch the other side of the zip. Press the fabric away from the stitching and close the zip. Stitch the remainder of the seam, then stitch tapes at the bottom.

147

Things to remember when inserting zips

1 A zipper foot allows you to stitch close to the coil.
2 Zip fastener lengths never include the tape ends.
3 If a zip is difficult to open lubricate it with candlewax, beeswax, or very carefully rub the lead of a pencil over the teeth.
4 Remember to check the temperature of the iron when pressing synthetic zips. Keep the zip closed for dry cleaning or washing.
5 Bias garments should hang overnight. A strip of seam binding on the wrong side of the fabric along the seam edge of the zip helps to avoid stretching.

6 Check the opening edges of each zip before inserting.
7 Always make sure the needle is centred over the notch of the foot.
8 A piece of sellotape placed to the cloth edge of the zip on the wrong side, so that half the tape edge comes outside, is a great help and serves as tacking. Take the side of the opening which is not stitched and stick it to the tape, putting the folded edge as close as possible.

Zips can be used as decorative trimmings as well as functional openings and with modern machines you will find instructions for using the swing needle to its full advantage.

Pressing garments

For successful dressmaking the pressing is most important and should be done as each section is completed, and hung up ready for the final assembly. When the garment is completed it is then 'pressed off'.

Pressing definitions
Under pressing: Done as the garment is made. For darts, pleats, tucks, facings etc.
Final pressing: When the garment is finished and pressed all over.
Top pressing: A touching-up process after the final pressing, ready for wear, display or dispatch.

Equipment used
Irons: There are various kinds, depending upon conditions, but they should always be clean and smooth.
Ironing boards: They must be adjusted to the correct height for the presser, firmly padded with no bumps or irregular surface and should have a stand for the iron so that the surface is not scorched.
Sleeve boards: These stand free of the main board and should be firmly padded.
Pressing cloths: Use old cotton pillowcases or pieces of cotton sheets, with no starch or dressing left in the fabric to stick to the iron.

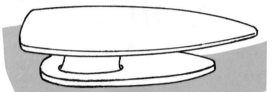

Dress pad: This is made of two oval pieces of material free from dressing, approximately 16 cm wide by 22 cm. It is used for pressing lace embroidery or shaped sections. Sometimes an old rolling pin padded and covered can be used.
A strip of card: Stiff card or doubled stiff brown paper will do for inserting between seams and the main garment.
Bowl of water: Useful if you have no steam iron.

Velvet or wire board: Used for pile cloths, especially velvets. It consists of a board set with vertical steel wires, like a brush. If a wire board is not available, a good firm clothes brush (clean) will answer the purpose.

Pressing various materials

Woollens Some fine worsteds have a tendency to shine. These should be steam-ironed until every part is free from shine. If the material has not been pre-shrunk, roll the length of cloth in a wet sheet. Always check for shrinkage before sewing. Use only a little steam for wool crêpe.

Pile fabrics Press lightly on a wire board with the cloth pile face down against the wires. They can also be steamed by using a steam kettle and brushing the fabric lightly, either with a brush or self material. Be careful not to crush the pile while wet and hang it to dry thoroughly afterwards.

Cotton and linens Press dark-coloured cottons and linens on the wrong side to prevent shining.

Silks Some silks and part silks can be pressed on the right side provided a press cloth is used. White silks must not be pressed with a hot iron, as they will change to a yellowy white.

Whenever possible use a pressing cloth.

Factory pressing equipment The type of equipment depends on whether the garments come into the category of light or heavy clothing. Light clothing firms use steam or tank irons, although pressing 'formers' are now fashionable. Hot air is released as the garments are on the formers, or shapes. Many firms still use Hoffman steam presses for heavy clothing although, again, modern firms tend to prefer hot air steam formers. The golden rule for pressing is 'press as you work', but here are some points for you to remember.

1 Always test the material and temperature of the iron first.
2 Press where there is a good light.
3 Whenever possible use a press cloth, whether pressing on the right or the wrong side.
4 Remember not to smooth the iron backwards and forwards as in ordinary ironing. Pressing means lifting and applying the iron to the part you are dealing with.
5 Do not press over pins, bound seams or tack marks.
6 Darts should be pressed flat and towards the centre front and centre back of garments. Horizontal darts are pressed downwards.

7 Thick bulky darts should be cut open and pressed flat.
8 Press with the grain.
9 Jersey fabrics should not be pressed across the width.
10 If the material has been dampened press it dry before removing it from the ironing board.
11 Make sure that all seams are not twisted and the garment is flat.
12 The pressing-off process covers all the final stages on the wrong side of the garment, in this order: (a) sleeves (b) bodice (c) skirt (d) collar (e) lapels.

Notes on tailoring

Before making any coat and jacket or tailored outfit, you must consider certain essentials. The materials must be suitable for the style and the occasion when the garment will be worn – for instance, town or country, summer or winter, formal or informal. Choose suitable interfacings for the cloth. Bonded or adhesive interfacings are not always suitable for woollen materials. Tailor's interfacings are usually of linen and haircloth. Linen is used in the revers, where the breakline or crease line occurs and is 'bridled' on this line to prevent stretching or gaping on that part of the body.

Haircloth is made of horsehair and is quite firm. It is used in the fronts of jackets and coats to hold the front of the scye and the shoulder firm.

Stay tape is applied to the front edges before the facings are sewn on. Collar canvas is used for the under-collar. Pad stitching helps to shape and control the roll of the collar.

Silesia is a material often used for pocket linings, although a firm cotton fabric will also serve. Sylvyt is a pocketing where warmth and a velvet texture are combined to produce a strong interlining. Domett is used for interlining where a specially warm coat is required. It is a soft fleecy material and is fixed to the lining before it is put into the coat. Fancy stitching can be used to hold it in position. A bias strip approximately 4 cm wide can be sewn to the crown of the sleeve seam to prevent any impression of the shoulder seam showing on the right side. Where silk facings are used domett is sandwiched between the facing to prevent the pad stitching showing on the right side.

Sewing threads Pure silk should be used in preference to anything else. A thick cord called *gimp* is used under the buttonhole twist in making buttonholes. It is rubbed through beeswax and twisted if a thicker cord is wanted. Buttonhole twist can be lightly waxed to prevent ravelling.

Material that has a gloss should be shrunk and pressed with a hot iron and very wet cloth. If this is not done at the beginning, a patchy effect may result.

Lingerie

Style influence
The design and cut of lingerie is greatly affected by what is worn over it. This applies especially to bridal gowns and to evening dresses, where flares are often repeated in the undergarments. Tailored overgarments demand tailored undergarments; full and flowing skirts need fullness in slips. Dainty undergarments can be most appealing, for children as well as adults.

Slips are usually 4 to 6 cm shorter than a dress.
Economy Choose materials of good quality and wash-and-wear properties with trimmings that will be durable and easily washable.

Advantages of slips They help to maintain the good line of the dress and protect and lengthen the life of the main garment.

Seams The type of seam is usually determined by the fabric. With silk jersey fabric the seams can be overlocked, but with a woven fabric which would necessitate cutting on the bias, the seams would be either French, run-and-fell or decorative stitching.

Trimming Edging of hems with lace, binding or decorative stitching will depend upon the material used.

Frills of lace and net are simple to attach. Lingerie lace with a net ground has a thread woven into the edge which will draw up, and it can be bought by the yard and in several widths.

Ribbon can be used as a decoration as well as for shoulder straps. Double satin ribbon is advisable for straps. Broderie anglaise is another pretty edging. In fact there are innumerable trimmings to choose from these days, but be careful not to select bulky edgings. They should be flat and suitable to the design and the fabric.

Clothes for children

Styles
The first consideration should be the comfort and happiness of the child who is wearing the garment. During the first few years fashion need not be followed to any great extent, and you will notice when looking at commercial patterns that the styles do not differ very much in cut and that variation is achieved mainly by materials and trimmings. If you look at ready-to-wear clothes for children you will find that they set an extremely high standard nowadays with many neat, pretty and even chic styles. There is no shortage of ideas for small garments that are both appealing and practical. For the older child and teenager the trend in dress among the particular age group should be taken as a general guide, as youngsters normally like to conform and to be up-to-date with current fashion in their age group.

Individual characteristics These should be taken into account when designing and making individual garments. The physical development, weight and height of a child must be considered, as they would be for grown-ups. The lengths for a chubby child should never be too short, the skirts too full or the trimmings too numerous. Fashion considerations should never be allowed to override one's good taste.

Using cast-off clothing If sufficient care is given to materials, cutting, and altering garments each child should be able to wear out her own clothes. However, there are times when an attractive coat and dress can be completely remade from the good material of an adult's coat or dress. It is not advisable to remake poor or worn fabric, but if care and interest is put into a garment, the results can be most worthwhile.

Colours and materials Provided light colours can be kept spotlessly clean for small children they are most attractive – white especially. Care must be taken when selecting cloths, as the garments are so much simpler in line, and construction. Mature women's fabrics would not be suitable for a very small child; large patterned prints and big flowery brocades would not really be suitable either, although they might appeal to a teenager. Cheerful, pretty, dainty fabrics should be chosen to produce youthful garments for little girls, while simple neat tailored patterns are best for boys.

Making patterns for children's garments Until the age of nine approximately the silhouette for a girl is almost straight, although younger children, both boys and girls, often appear to have a slightly corpulent line.

When cutting patterns for children remember that once the neckline and armhole has been patterned and shaped and the block pattern is made, the remainder of the garment is simple, so long as the basic proportions are retained.

A child's trousers can be cut as for those of a grown-up, provided the correct measurements are taken. Trousers can be cut with or without side seams, the waistline facing can be grown-on, and elastic inserted at the waist to allow for easy pull-on and off movements.

Boys' clothes often have sleeves of the set-in or raglan types. They can be single or double-breasted, belted or unbelted and involve practically the same construction details as adult clothes.

Girls' knickers or panties can be cut on the same lines as adults', but children's underwear should harmonise as much as possible with the dress and trimmings should be dainty and durable. The reason is that such garments are never entirely concealed on little girls.

The chief aim is to provide warmth, and the first clothes should be made with ample room to allow for growth. They should be light and all seams should be as flat as possible, as any bumps will irritate the skin. All materials should be smooth and have no irritating qualities, while the colours should not be too strong for tiny children.

The following points should be borne in mind before making any children's garments:

1. Garments should permit freedom for active movement and flares, pleats, tucks and gathers should allow for this.
2. Garments should have front openings where possible. If neck and waist openings are used they should be large enough to ensure ease of dressing. 'Self help' garments for the very young should have long openings, large buttons and fastenings, ample armholes and necks, while the backs of garments should be easily distinguishable from the front. Trousers are easier for handling when there is no fly and the pants can be pulled down easily, especially if the legs are not tight.
3. Allow good turn-ups on hems for lengthening. This applies to sleeves also. Hems and sleeve lengths usually follow the natural fashion trends and vary considerably. Good seam allowances are always advisable.
4. Garments should be made of washable fabrics as far as possible.
5. Fabrics should be light in weight and yet strong enough to allow for hard wear. The materials should not be rough or heavy.
6. Garments should, where possible, be designed so that they need the minimum amount of care.
7. Patterns and colours of children's garments should be in keeping with the likes and dislikes of the age group.
8. Trimming on children's clothing should be simple, easily cared for, colourfast to washing and sun and firmly stitched. Flat functional buttons should be sewn to the garment and there should be no sharp edges to cut and injure the child.
9. All garments should be reinforced at the places of greatest strain – underarm seams, forks and knees of trousers – while the edges with the greatest amount of wear should be reinforced with facings or rows of stitching.
10. To prevent pulling out at the waistline of shirts and blouses, ample tails should be provided. All dresses, shirts and blouses should be easy across the back. Sleeves should be easy to get into and out of and there should be no restriction across arm bands, which should be large enough to prevent tearing. The whole garment should be comfortable.

Leather garments

Care must be taken when selecting a skin, but always choose a good leather. Hold up the skin to the light and choose one of even thickness, and test the stretch of the skin in the centre, where the spine was. Select a smooth-finished skin if you require one that will not soil easily. It is sometimes advisable to cut duplicates of the pattern and arrange these on the skin to check the layout. The commonest hand stitch used is stab stitch and it should be even.

Points to remember when machining leather
1   It is advisable to try sections cut in felt first if you are unsure of the fit.
2   Mark on the wrong side with chalk. Do not tack.
3   Instead of tacking use paper clips or masking tape.
4   Cut with large sharp shears, a razor blade or a Stanley knife.
5   Use rubber cement to stick sections and seams, but not where it will be obvious.
6   Skive, i.e. split leathers where they overlap.
7   Do not select weak parts of the leather for places where stress will occur.
8   Do not ease unless the leather is very soft and pliable.
9   Shiny leather may need tissue paper, as for chiffons and silks.
10 Masking tape will hold seams ready for stitching.
11 Shiny leathers machine better if sewing machine oil is lightly smoothed on the surface before machining. Always test first.
12 When choosing seams consider the fabric. Heavyweight leathers need overlapped seams. Lightweight leathers need traditional seaming. Soft leathers need narrow seams. Thick leather (cowhide) needs wider seam stitches with buttonhole twist.
13 Use a glover's needle and silk thread, coating the thread by drawing through beeswax to prevent tangling.
14 Short stitches will perforate and weaken the skin, causing the garment to tear at the seams.
15 Stitch from neck to hem for long seams.
16 Do not back-stitch – it may cause the leather to tear.
17 It is not advisable to stitch too fast. Finish seams by tying the ends.
18 To make circular or curved hems smooth, cut triangular pieces from the hem.

One should always take into account that the majority of leathers have very little flexibility, so that garments should be cut to allow for this. Remember that close-fitted sleeves are not advisable for leather.

Quality standards

Know value and quality

A garment can be judged by the way it is cut, sewn and finished (this includes the final pressing) and by the trimmings used. Clothes cut with the grain wear and hang better, while materials, handwork and style affect the price of the garment. An exclusive design will naturally be much more expensive than a garment 'off the peg'. Be discerning, not impulsive, when buying.

Consider carefully and decide whether:
1   The purchase would be an asset to the wardrobe.
2   Will it give good service?
3   Is it easy to care for?
4   Is it good value for the price?
5   Does it improve your appearance?

Then look at the garment for quality, price, style, labels and guarantees. Prices will vary according to the overhead expenses and turnover.

Recognising quality in garments
First of all, know what you want and do not let sales talk influence your purchase. Bear in mind the following points:
1   Bonded fabrics often come 'unbonded' after several cleanings.
2   A firmly woven cloth usually gives better wear than a loosely woven one.
3   Good seams should be allowed on materials which fray and the finish should be appropriate to the cloth.
4   Hems should be invisible and no ridge or shine should show on the right side of the garment.

5 Collars should be placed so that both sides are symmetrical (unless the design is deliberately asymmetrical). The under-collar should not be visible on the right side.

6 Sleeves should not pull on the figure, there should be no signs of puckering and they should be set in smoothly.

7 Lapels should lie flat and should not gape.

8 Fasteners should be securely attached and should match the garment. An extra button should be attached for replacement.

9 Decoration and trim should be of good quality.

10 Plaids and patterned fabrics should match at the seams wherever possible.

11 There should be no seam puckering, and the threads should match the material.

12 Pockets and openings should be reinforced, as should buttonholes.

13 Velvets and pile fabrics should be checked for incorrect cutting and shading.

14 If there is dragging across a garment, check the linings, and interfacings for the cause of the distortion.

15 Linings should not hang below the hems or below the sleeves.

16 Check the grain line on the garment and see that the fronts and backs hang straight.

17 Look for fabric faults.

18 Look for pieces in the fork of the trousers and check that there is adequate seat fullness.

19 On good quality garments, check that inside seams have sufficient extra material for letting out.

20 Finally read the label carefully for all the details of the fabric.

Faults in manufacture These can be caused by uneven seams, incorrect grain lines, the omission of notches and balance marks, failure to pair parts, mixing of sizes and colours, mixing of dye lots and fabric faults missed when laying up.

Faults in making-up These include darts incorrectly machined, wrong seam allowances taken, uneven seams, sleeves inserted in the wrong armhole, and skirt sections incorrectly placed. Sometimes garments are incorrectly pressed, cuff seams and collar seams show, hems are not pressed (or pressed too hard so that a ridge is created). No doubt you could give a list yourself.

A final word of warning: be wary of sales garments. Check these carefully before purchasing for shading and for any of the faults previously mentioned. Remember you cannot return sales goods in many stores and it is not a bargain if you cannot wear the garment. Under normal conditions, if faults are detected, return the goods to the manufacturer. This will ensure that standards of quality are maintained.

Final advice

Set yourself high standards, be prepared to devote time, perseverance, patience and imagination, and pay attention to all the details discussed in this book. Your rewards will be enormous in the steady increase of your knowledge and practical skills and the satisfaction of having mastered a craft.

GLOSSARY

Abnet – Long scarf or sash, usually of linen.

Accessory – Article of clothing that completes an outfit such as gloves, hats, bags, jewelry, belts, neckwear, buttons, scarfs etc.

Accordion pleating – Pleating the material in even folds to resemble those of an accordion.

Ada – Coarse open canvas.

Adaptation – Garment similar to an original model yet having distinct changes in methods of making, material trimmings etc.

Adjusting the pattern – The altering of a pattern after the first trial sample has been cut and made, i.e. it may need to be made smaller or larger, according to the nature of the cloth.

Afghaline – Light weight wool crêpe.

Afghan – Soft wool blanket, usually knitted or crocheted. Used as a coverlet or worn as wrap.

A la mode – French phrase meaning 'in fashion' or 'according to fashion'.

'A' Line – Christian Dior produced a line in 1955 which had fairly narrow shoulders and bust and a wide hemline at low calf length. The horizontal line of the 'A' came approximately at the knees, from which sprang extra fullness in pleats, flares or flounces.

Alpaca – Coat of the alpaca, a variety of llama.

Angel Sleeve – Long loose flowing sleeve.

Appliqué – A cut-out design, applied to another piece of fabric by stitching, embroidery or adhesive.

Apron Tunic – Long or short, usually sleeveless, open ornamental tunic worn apron-fashion.

Arrowhead – Used to secure the top of a pleat or at the end of a pocket.

Artificial (or art) silk – An old name for rayon.

Assembling – A machinist attaches the garment pieces together, i.e. assembles it, by means of corresponding notches in each section.

Astrakhan – Wool or lamb's fur of a curly nature coming from Astrakhan in Russia.

Baize – A coarse open cloth.

Balance – The adjustment of back and front garment lengths, to suit the natural position of the figure. Left and right sides of both back and front of the garment sections are usually equal.

Balance marks – Notches put in pattern sections preserve the balance of the garment during making. Usually in the centre front and centre back armholes, sleeve head, side seams and underarm seams.

Bannockburn tweed – Woollen cloth used for suits and trousers, woven with alternate threads of mottled and solid colour threads.

Barathea – A ribbed hopsack weave, hard wearing, crease resisting. Used for coats and suits.

Bar tacks – Worked by hand. Used on sheer fabrics instead of a metal eye or used to strengthen the end of an opening.

Basic cuts – Classic lines, e.g. the princess and the sheath, that follow the line of the body but have no added style features.

Basting – Otherwise known as tacking. Used to join two pieces of fabric together temporarily with a large open hand stitch.

Bateau, Boat Neck – Neckline following the curved shape of the collar bone, giving a scooped effect. The neck points are cut away and the effect is wide and slightly curved.

Batiste – A light soft thin, plain woven fabric. Used primarily for shirts and handkerchiefs.

Bell – Stiffened skirt, bell shape. The skirt springs from waist level, just above or even below the waistline.

Bengaline – A crosswise ribbed fabric. Used for dresses and suits etc. medium weight.

Bespoke – Technical name for garments, usually outerwear, cut to individual measurements and requirements. A bespoke tailor may employ a cutter and operatives to work in his premises.

Bias – Slantwise. The effect of folding fabric on a line diagonal to the grain. The weft threads are made to run in the same direction as the warp threads.

Blend – The combining of different fibres in one fabric, e.g. wool and silk, which produce a warm light material. Blending achieves economy (using less of the more expensive component and substituting a cheaper fibre), shape retention (as in permanently pleated fabrics with Terylene or Tricel added) and better handling qualities (as in velvet with viscose rayon and nylon added).

Block pattern – Master pattern or basic pattern made to a set of individual measurements, or in standard sizes for mass production. Consists of skirt, bodice (front and back) and sleeve. These five sections are completely plain, having only the basic darts.

Blouses – Separate garment covering the top part of the body. Can be fastened down the back, front, side and shoulders. Worn tucked in at the waist or as over-blouse. Can be frilly and feminine or severely tailored, according to taste.

Bouclé – A curled or looped effect on many materials.

Bridle – A strip of linen pad stitched to the canvas to prevent stretching along the roll of the lapel. Used in tailored garments.

Broadcloth – A fine, tightly woven woollen cloth having a twill back and a napped surface. Originally woven very wide to allow for shrinkage – hence its name.

Brushed fabric – A fabric in which the loose fibres are brushed and brought to the surface.

Bulked multifilament – A thread treated to produce crimped filaments. Used where stretch is required, for swimwear etc.

Burr or nylon tape – Tapes from synthetic fibres with tiny hooks on one side and fleece on the other. When pressed together the hooks cling to the fleece effecting a closure. Trade name 'Velcro'.

'Butch' – Masculine, slough hats, tailored slacks etc. Sometimes called the 'Gangster Look'. Late 1950's.

Cabbage – A slang term meaning the larger pieces of material left over after cutting the garments.

Caftan – Collarless, slit-neck, long flowing robe, loose wide sleeves. Decorative trim slit at sides. Based on a Biblical garment.

Calendering – A process giving surface polish to a fabric.

Calico – Plain woven cotton with slightly stiff dressing which washes out. Obtainable bleached or unbleached. Originally made in Calicut, India.

Cambric – Fine lightweight fabric used for lingerie and blouses, but also made in a narrow width, with a slight dressing and calendered (glazed) one side; often used for pocket linings. Originally made in Cambrai, France.

Camouflage – Concealing the true appearance by disguise. Many poor body shapes can be skilfully camouflaged whether by cloth texture, colour or the clever use of lines.

Cape – Sleeveless over-garment of varying length, having slits for the arms. Gives a smooth, clean appearance over the shoulder line. Can be cut with seams over the shoulder running parallel to front and back.

Cardigan – Jacket, generally teamed with sweaters. Usually buttoned or zipped down the front. A separate strip edging is often used. This method of finishing the neckline and opening is also found on cardigan-styled dresses.

Cashmere – Very soft and warm fabric made from the wool of the Kashmir goat.

Casing – A small hem with an opening so that tape or elastic or ribbon can be inserted.

Cavalry twill – A thick heavy fabric with a prominent diagonal double rib.

Centralise – The placing of a pattern on the exact centre of a check or stripe, i.e. the line denoting the centre of the panel.

Chanel Cardigan – Originally a simple wool knit, unfitted or semi-fitted casually styled cardigan type jacket, hip length worn with a simple skirt and soft blouse. First introduced in 1919.

Chaser – A person who checks on progress or 'chases' special orders in a factory to keep them up to time.

Chemise (or shift) – A straight, unbelted smock-type garment, fitted to the bust.

Cheongsam – Full-length, long sleeved robe straight cut, slit to the side at one side. Mandarin collar, diagonal opening from centre front neck.

Chiffon – A sheer plain-weave lightweight fabric. Used for evening wear, lingerie and flimsy blouses.

Classic Garment – Garment with no definite current style feature. Apart from length and proportions they can be worn season after season. Not usually extreme or exaggerated in cut. Basically simple, it fulfils the needs of the bulk of the buying public. If a classic design is good, it will remain virtually timeless and in fashion.

Cloqué – Double fabric with a blistered or cockled effect.

C.M.T. – In the trade this means Cut, Make and Trim. Many small firms do not design or buy the material but manufacture for larger firms.

Coat dress – Buttoned-through formal dress, tailored in appearance. Usually with a collar and made up in a firm fabric.

Coat tabs. – Loops made from lining, for hanging garments on hooks. A firm cord may be inserted for strengthening.

Cocktail dress – Short formal dress for early evening wear. Now declining in popularity. Made in many fabrics, from plain crêpe to elaborately glittered material. Often with embroidery, beads and other decorations. An alternative

is the tunic and trouser suit or the more informal type of long evening wear.

Collar – Shaped part of a garment that completes the upper neck section. Can stand upright against the neck or roll over into a dress, coat or any type of garment. May be attached or detached.

Collection – Fashion designs shown to the press, wholesale buyers and private clients. Couture houses usually show spring and summer collections in January and autumn and winter collections in August. Wholesale houses show spring and summer collections in October or November and autumn and winter collections in May or early June. Retail stores are usually a little later.

Corduroy – Woven velveteen with ribs of pile running lengthways. Can be cut either all up or all down the pile, whichever gives the darker effect. Used for trouser suits and riding breeches.

Corsage – A bodice shaped to the figure as the foundation for a strapless dress. Bone or metal strips are shaped and inserted into the seam lines.

Costing – An estimate of the total cost of producing a garment, based on the price of material, trimmings, zips, linings, etc. and also labour and overheads.

Couture – Literally the French word for 'needlework'. A term used for high class garments, individually designed and fitted. Couture clothes produced by famous fashion houses are considered the ultimate in style and finish. The quality of the material and the care that goes into the making are reflected in the very high price.

Crêpe – General term used for fabric with a crinkled or wrinkled effect. Drapes well but has a tendency to shrink.

Cuffs – Finishes to sleeves or trouser bottoms. They can be sewn on, grown on or detachable.

Cutter – In bespoke tailoring: someone who takes the measurements and cuts the pattern. In the wholesale garment trade: someone who cuts with an electric cutter, shears or band knife.

Cutter or Trimmer – A worker employed to mark up cloth, linings or other material and to lay up cloth, separate the parts of the garments after they have been cut and assemble the bundles for the machinist.

Damask – A figured fabric, originally in warp and weft satin weave, used for table linen. Named after Damascus.

Darts – A means of shaping material to fit the body. Stitched folds, tapered to a point which should end towards the fullest part of the bulge.

Demi-Tailleur – A half tailored style produced by a dressmaker using a mixture of tailoring and dressmaking methods.

Denim – A coarse and firmly woven twill, originally '*serge de Nîmes*', from the town in France. The warp thread is usually coloured while the weft is white. Strong, hard-wearing, used for jeans, skirts, suits, etc.

Design – An arrangement of lines, shapes, cloth, texture and colour to give a distinctive overall effect. Structural design is the putting together of all sections, skirt, bodice, sleeves, etc. of a garment.

Design – Applied – An addition to a garment in the form of trimming, e.g. buttons, beading, appliqué, embroidery, braid, piping, lace, ribbon, flowers.

Designer – A creator and innovator of fashion. Essentially he or she should bring the stimulus of fresh ideas to the work, because fashion is continually changing and evolving.

Differential Feed – A means of controlling the feeding through of material on a sewing machine. With the aid of special feed dogs fabric can be stretched or gathered.

Dimity – Sheer, crisp cotton fabric with soft lustre, made from mercerised yarn.

Dior slit or pleat – An opening at the centre back of a skirt or dress, extending about 16 cm or more from the hemline. Lying behind it and attached to the lining is a piece of the same material as the skirt.

Directoire or Empire – High waisted style of dress emphasising the bust and with neat, simple sleeves. A feature is made of the neckline. Skirts are soft and slightly gathered. Copied from Grecian and Roman period ladies' dresses.

Direct Application System – A system found in the wholesale trade. A workroom stand is marked with the main construction lines used for drafting a block pattern. The sections are measured and applied to the draft without the use of a scale or proportions.

Direct Measurement System – A method of taking measurements directly from a figure and applying them to the draft.

Dirndl – A very full skirt gathered into a tight waistband.

Dolman – A lady's mantle with armholes. Patterned originally after a long Turkish outer garment. It has a wing-like silhouette. The sleeve usually has a seam running over the shoulder low down on to the front and back bodice of the garment. The armhole is deep and can be curved or square.

Dolman sleeve – A one-piece sleeve cut with a deep scye. The armholes can be round or square.

Double edge – The folded edge midway between the selvedges when the length of cloth is folded down the middle.

Draft – A plan of a garment. Blocks have to be manipulated on a flat piece of paper to correspond with the design and superimposed ready for tracing on to the pattern paper. Balance marks and notches are indicated. The traced pattern is cut and finalised, ready for the sample garment to be cut.

Draping – A method of producing a pattern immediately by laying material on a model or figure and pinning, cutting, folding etc. to the shape.

Duck – Heavy cotton in plain weave. Lighter and finer than canvas.

Ease or Easing – A means of fitting pattern sections together when one seam edge is longer than the other, as in the head of a sleeve. The surplus is eased or lightly gathered in between certain points and notches.

Ease of movement – Extra allowance made in certain parts of the pattern to provide additional room for movement.

Ensemble – Two-piece or three-piece including all accessories.

Fad – Usually a passing craze, but occasionally a fad is adopted. Recent fads have been pedal pushers, bell-bottom trousers and coloured hosiery, which today are now accepted as fashion.

Faille – Ribbed fabric like grosgrain but the ribs are wider and flatter. The rib is crossways or weftwise. Used for dresses, coats and suits.

Fitting – The process of making a garment suit the shape of the wearer in a normal comfortable position. There should be no unnecessary wrinkles or appearance of tightness.

Flaws – Faults in the weaving and making of fabrics, e.g. the slippage of threads in making, tears, holes, misprints, etc.

Fraying – The slippage of threads in weaving which causes a fringed appearance in the material.

French dart – A type of dart where waist and shoulder darts are joined together and run from the centre shoulder to the waist over the point of the bust.

French tack – A loose large tacking stitch for holding two pieces of fabric together. Used to attach linings to the hems of coats or for cowls.

Frock – An outer garment. Dresses are often referred to as 'frocks'. Originally a priest's gown with long loose sleeves.

Fusing – A process of applying one material to another by the application of chemicals and heat, for example, for interfacings.

Georgette – A fine light fabric, made with crêpe yarns. Used for trimmings and lingerie.

Gilet – A waistcoat or vest.

Gingham – Used for blouses, shirts and dresses. A hard-wearing fabric, woven sometimes in coloured yarns, often in checks, a summer lightweight material.

Godet – An insert into a seam or cut.

Gore – A shaped panel in a skirt or coat.

Grading – A means of increasing and decreasing pattern sizes to suit individual firms. It can be done by hand or machine or computer and is a regular mathematical increase and decrease in each dimension of length and girth, divided into the correct sections of the body.

Grain – The warp, selvedge or lengthwise thread of the material, recognised as the stronger thread. (The weft is usually a little more elastic.)

Grosgrain – Closely woven fabric with fine ribs running across it. Similar to petersham ribbon. Used for evening wear and for suits.

Gusset – A section of material inserted to allow more ease of movement, usually under the arm of sleeves. It can be any shape, according to the design.

Handle – To feel and test for thickness, softness, creasing, draping and flexibility in the cloth.

Inlay – Extra cloth left in seams for enlargements.

Interfacings – Shaped pieces inserted between two pieces of cloth to give shape, e.g. pocket flaps, collars, revers etc. See also 'interlinings' below.

Interlinings – Pieces of fabric inserted between the main body of the garment and the lining to give extra warmth or body shaping. Nowadays the word is also often used to describe interfacings.

Jabot – A frilled neckpiece worn at the front.

Jersey – A knitted fabric, circular or flat. May be silk, wool or synthetic. Drapes well and is used for all types of dresses. Also used for swimwear, lingerie, suits and coats.

Jetting – Piping on pockets.

Kimono – A sleeved garment with the sleeve cut all in one with the main body. Modern kimono cuts have a seam down the centre of the sleeve.

Lamé – A material used for evening wear. A combination of a metal warp and silk or other fibre weft. Also made with a cotton warp and a rayon weft.

Lapel – The turn-back on a dress, jacket or coat, between the top button and the collar.

Lap for buttonholes – The amount of fabric on the button-hole side of the garment, from the centre line of the buttons to the edge of the closing, is the overlap. Underlap is the amount of fabric on the button side beyond the centre line of the buttons.

Lawn – A light plain woven fabric, originally from Laon, France. Thin and fine and sometimes stiffened. Used for children's clothes, lingerie, blouses and dresses.

Layer – To reduce the bulk of seams where the seam allowances are cut in different widths so that a smoother and flatter appearance results.

Layout or 'Lay' – The arrangement of pattern pieces on a length of paper of the same width as the fabric. Sections are moved about to achieve most economical setting out. For very large layouts, many firms have special equipment. Such machines, usually miniature scale, save time and labour.

Leaf edge – The thin outer edge of a collar.

Line placement – The correct positioning of the design lines on the pattern. A good knowledge of the shapings of the body is required. Seam lines should be placed to emphasise the good points of the figure and minimise the bad ones.

Madras – A soft fabric, originating in India, used for blouses, dresses, shirtings and children's wear. Many fancy effects are obtained in weaving, on a plain background.

Magyar sleeve – A sleeve cut in one with the bodice and with a gusset or wedge shape let in under the arm.

Manufacturing systems – Garment manufacture is organised on one of the following systems: bundle, progressive bundle, conveyor belt, make-through, section work or synchro-flo.

Marker – A long sheet of (spot and cross) paper, on which the layout is already marked for cutting. Several types of machine will copy markers from the original layout ready for cutting. Also applies to hand markers for any special stitching, buttonholes, etc.

Mohair – Fine soft silky hair of the angora goat bred in South Africa. Often blended with wool or other fibres to make a long-haired fabric. The fibres are characterised by their strength and lustre and are clearly separable.

Moiré – A ribbed fabric with a watermarked appearance. A rippled effect.

Moulded garments – A form of pressing and shaping complete garments, tried by Molyneux in 1930. Experiments in 1969 produced a tubular knitted fabric heat-shrunk on to a mould like the human figure and then overcured to keep its shape during washing and wearing. Advantages were smart appearance and minimal wastage. Disadvantages were the difficulty of disguising figure faults.

Nainsook – Light soft plain woven fabric, made from mercerised yarn. May be calendered one side. Used for children's garments and lingerie.

Nankeen – A cotton cloth of dull yellowish colour, the natural hue of the cotton from which it is made. The name comes from Nanking in China. Much of the Nankeen cloth is made in Lancashire with ordinary cotton and dyed the same shade as the original.

Nap – The surface of the fabric. A fabric which requires a 'one-way layout', e.g. a cloth with a pile, or even a satin.

Neck point – An imaginary line drawn from the lobe of the ear down to the base of the neck gives the neck point. The shoulder seam is normally fitted along the highest edge of the shoulder to the neck point.

Needlecord – Fabric similar to corduroy but made in a finer rib and lighter weight. Used for children's and adults' garments and dresses.

Noil – Yarn spun from the lowest grade of silk or other fibres. Waste produced in the early stages of silk manufacture.

Notches – Indentations made as a guide for the easy assembly of the garment. They are clipped into the pattern to provide the balance points to denote seam allowances.

Nub – Man-made fibre of mineral origin.

Oldham – A rough worsted cloth from Oldham, Lancs.

Ombré – A fabric with a shaded effect obtained by using different dyed yarns when weaving.

Open – (Applied to trousers) Cut in a particular way for an open stance.

Organdie – A crisp transparent fabric. Closely woven in a weave from very fine yarn. Used for blouses, dresses and interlinings. Can be coloured and embroidered and made permanently crisp.

Organza – Similar to organdie but not so crisp or wiry. A sheer fabric used for evening wear and blouses.

Ottoman – A cross-corded fabric similar to faille and grosgrain but having larger and rounder ribs. Used for coats and suits.

Overcheck – Another check introduced over a basic check producing a double check effect.

Overcutting – Cutting more garments than are required.

Overlocking – A machine stitch which oversews and locks the edges of material. Used to prevent the fraying of raw edges.

Overspun yarn – A faulty yarn where the material is thinner in places. This is caused by too much twist.

Paisley – An elaborate Persian pine-cone pattern which originated in Paisley, Scotland.

Panama – A smooth fabric like nuns' veiling but heavier.

Panne velvet – A flattened pile velvet used at one time for millinery.

Passer – An employee who checks and examines garments in the clothing trade.

Pattern-cutter – An employee who converts fashion ideas and styles into patterns.

Pattern-grader – A producer of patterns in a range of different sizes. Must have a knowledge of figure shapings.

Peau de Soie – A heavy satin material used for evening wear and wedding gowns.

Peplum – A flared, pleated or fitted extension to a jacket or bodice which is attached and seamed around the waistline which is close fitting. The hemline can be varied or graduated, possibly from very short in front to longer at back.

Perching – The drawing of a fabric piece over a long roller or 'perch' before it is finished. Faults are shown up at that stage.

Picking – A weaving term for the operation of projecting the shuttle from one side of the loom to the other.

Picot – A means of edging which can be produced by a hemstitching machine. The cloth is hemstitched and then cut between the hem and stitching to produce a small looped effect. It can also be woven into the edge of ribbon and is seen on the edge of lace.

Piece – A length of cloth from 27 to 91 metres (30 to 100 yards). Most British manufacturers supply pieces of 36·5 to 54·8 metres (40 to 60 yards). Buyers generally specify a minimum piece size to cut down waste in production and receive a 'cut through' allowance for those which fall short.

Piqué – A firm medium-weight cotton fabric with a raised pattern either in honeycomb, cord or rib. Used for blouses, dresses and sportswear.

Placket – An opening in a garment, to allow ease of taking on and off. It may be fastened with a zip, buttons, press studs, ties, hooks and eyes or other method.

Plastron – A breast pad used for building up thin figures. Also a half-blouse for wearing under jackets.

Pleating – The creasing and pressing of material into folds. Flat or knife pleats: folds face in one direction. Box pleats: alternate folds face in opposite directions. Inverted pleats: two knife pleats face each other to meet in the centre. Crystal pleats: very small accordion pleating. Vandyke pleats: as accordion pleats but giving a V effect. Sunray: similar to accordion but radiating from a common point. French combination pleating: varied groups of flat, box or inverted pleats. Goffering: like crystal pleating, but with a rounded edge.

Pleating a skirt – Cloth is cut, hemmed, etc. and then sandwiched between two layers of firm paper which have been creased to the shape of the pleats. It is then concertina-ed, rolled and tied, subjected to pressure and steam in an oven. After cooling and drying the pattern is removed.

Plissé – A puckered cotton fabric like seersucker, but finer.

Plush – A cut pile fabric like velvet but with a greater depth of pile.

Pongee – Made from wild silk. A plain woven fabric with a slub effect. Used for blouses and dresses.

Poplin – A firm medium-weight cotton from mercerised cotton yarn. Fine ribbed effect. Washes well Can have a drip-dry finish.

Poult – A plain woven fabric, similar to taffeta but heavier. Weft threads thicker than the warp produce a ribbed effect. Used for evening wear.

Pre-shrinking – Treatment of materials to shrink the cloth before use. Water is sprayed on before the finishing process.

Pressure foot – A device on a sewing machine to produce an even flow of material.

Print – A general term for fabric stamped with a design. The dye is used on wood blocks, rolled on silk screens and stamped on to the material in various ways.

Profile stitching – A technique whereby material to be sewn is placed under a shaped template. The firm edge acts as a guide for the needle and helps the operator.

Proportionate measurement system – A system based on typical proportions of people of various heights and types of figure. These average measurements are obtained by statistical analysis.

Quality control – A system of inspection devised to keep a good standard of workmanship in garment manufacturing.

Quilting – A method of sewing two layers of material together with a soft interlining. Patterned effects are produced.

Raising – Fabric fibres are raised to the surface by a machine process to give a thicker effect.

Rayon – A man-made fibre, wholly or mainly of cellulose. Can imitate the appearance and characteristics of many other fabrics, such as brocade, bouclé, crêpe, gabardine, jersey etc.

Saddle stitch – A bold decoration, type of running stitch, used to outline collars or any seams. Also used for making gloves.

Sailcloth – Strong, firm canvas-type cotton fabric made in various weights. Used for trousers and sportswear.

Sanforized – A registered trade mark declaring that the material has been subject to controlled compression shrinkage. The process can be used on all cottons and linens and many rayon fabrics.

Repp – A cotton fabric in various weights, with distinct ribs running across caused by heavy weft threads.

Ruching – A method of making a frilly edging. This can be gathered in a normal way, shell gathered or heart-shaped.

Sample – An original design made up by a firm and patterned to suit its production methods. When the sample is copied in small quantities for the agents, each copy is called a duplicate.

Sarcenet — A fine soft fabric, plain or twill.

Sateen – A fabric, usually cotton, with a glossy finish resembling satin.

Satin – A closely-woven silk-type fabric made with a satin weave and having a lustrous smooth surface. Types include crêpe, panne, duchess, slipper, lining, upholstery, wash satin and the least rich of the satin family, paillette.

Satin finish – A finish given to materials to imitate satin, a highly glossed and lustrous effect.

Satinising – A silk-like gloss applied to cotton fabrics by impregnating them with a salt solution.

Scalloping – A series of semi-circles created by stitching as an edge decoration.

Scye – An old English word for armhole.

Seat angle – Refers to trouser-making. This angle regulates the amount of ease in the seat or underside.

Seersucker – Cotton fabric with puckered lengthways stripes. Does not need ironing.

Selvedge – The unfrayable edge of a fabric where weft and warp threads interlace.

Shaping – The moulding of a garment section into shape by pressing, using heat and steam.

Shapings – The re-cutting of garment sections, using a template or shaper.

Shoulder pad – A soft pad shaped to fit the shoulder to accentuate a prevailing fashion line.

Shuttle – The device which carries the weft across the loom in weaving.

Slopers – Another name for templates.

Squaring a line – Drawing a line at right angles (90°) to another line. Place the set square against one line to draw a square, or part of a square.

Stay patches – Patches of fabric (adhesive or non adhesive) used where extra strength is required, e.g. the backs of buttons, corners of gussets, at collars and cuff points to prevent curling, at corners of pockets, backs of pleats, etc.

Stay stitching – A holding stitch used in the early stages of garment assembly to prevent stretching, for example on a neckline, pocket flaps or collars. An extra row of stitching to tighten an edge on the wrong side.

Stay tapes – Cut lengths of tape or cloth applied to the shoulder seams or waists of garments to prevent stretching. Used especially with jersey fabrics.

Steam air-form finishers – Specially shaped nylon bags over which the garments are put to be steam pressed. The bags are inflated with hot air and steam away any creases. Fabrics should be tested first for heat, colour, shrinkage, stretch, spottings and surface change.

Surah – A twill weave silk fabric, soft and lustrous. Used for blouses and dresses.

Swatch – Small pieces of material, placed in order of shade and colour. Used by textile or clothing firms to show their range of fabrics.

Taffeta – A slightly stiff silk or similar fabric, plain woven with the weft thicker than the warp. Used for linings, petticoats and evening wear.

Tailor's chalk – A special fine chalk for marking cloth. Available in white and colours, though white is easier to remove and is advised for sheer and flimsy materials.

Teazle (teasel) – A prickly burr used to tease the nap on cloth.

Terry towelling – A cotton fabric much used for beach wear, dressing gowns and clothes for young children. Woven with shaggy loops. Also available as a stretch fabric.

Texture – The surface 'feel' of cloth.

Time-study – Assessment of the time a job should ideally take, based on scientific observation.

Tobralco – Light cotton fabric in a haircord weave. Hard wearing and washes well.

Toile – A preliminary pattern for a model garment made from a cotton fabric of the same weight as the material it represents.

Tolerance – An allowance for body movement and comfort in a garment by the provision of extra material in places where it is needed.

True-up – The process of correcting lines on a garment pattern, by rulers, curves and set squares. Traced lines on a pattern may be uneven, or curves not smooth enough. Darts should be folded in the correct direction, and seam lines checked in length and depth.

Tussore – Wild silk fabric in a plain weave. Light, crisp and used for blouses and dresses.

Tweed – A heavy woven woollen fabric with a rough hairy surface.

Twill – A generic name for basic weave fabrics with a diagonal rib.

Velvet – A silk fabric with a short, thick pile.

Velveteen – Cotton-based fabric with a mercerised weft pile. A short pile fabric. Resembles velvet. Used for children's wear and dresses.

Vicuna – Fabric made from hair of the wild llama of South America.

Voile – A sheer muslin-like fabric made from tightly twisted yarn, often with raised dots woven into it. Suitable for blouses, dresses and babies' wear.

Warp – The lengthwise thread of a fabric, running parallel to the selvedge.

Welding – A method of joining garment sections other than by sewing. Raincoats and waterproof garments may be welded, though are often stitched first to meet government regulations on waterproofing. Welding has been tried on corsetry, ladies' crimplene trousers and the applying of pockets to overalls. The technique is still in the early stages. Its advantages are speed and the prevention of fraying, its drawback the impossibility of altering if incorrectly done.

Winceyette – Hard wearing fabric used for night wear. A warm cotton fabric, soft with a brushed surface. Highly flammable unless treated with a flame-resistant finish.

Woof – Another name for the weft or crosswise thread.

Wool – The hair from sheep, lambs and other animals, spun, woven, knitted or felted into fabrics for clothing.

Wool dyed – Dyed in the wool before weaving.

Worsted – A smooth-handling woollen fabric produced from long fibres, woven with a stronger twist than other woollens and therefore a strong fabric.